The Prison Reform Movement

FORLORN
HOPE

SOCIAL MOVEMENTS PAST AND PRESENT

Irwin T. Sanders, Editor

The Prison Reform Movement

FORLORN
HOPE

Larry E. Sullivan

Twayne Publishers • Boston
A Division of G. K. Hall & Co.

The Prison Reform Movement: Forlorn Hope
Larry E. Sullivan

Copyright 1990 by G. K. Hall & Co.
All rights reserved.
Published by Twayne Publishers
A division of G. K. Hall & Co.
70 Lincoln Street, Boston, Massachusetts 02111

Copyediting supervised by Barbara Sutton.
Book Production by Janet Z. Reynolds.
Typeset by Compset, Inc., of Beverly, Massachusetts.

Printed on permanent/durable acid-free paper
and bound in the United States of America.

Library of Congress Cataloging-in-Publication Data

Sullivan, Larry E.
The prison reform movement : forlorn hope / Larry E. Sullivan.
p.   cm.—(Social movements past and present)
Includes bibliographical references.
ISBN 0-8057-9739-4.—ISBN 0-8057-9740-8 (pbk.)
1. Prisons—United States. I. Title. II. Series.
HV9469.S86   1990
365′.7′0973—dc20   89-27488
                                                     CIP

ISBN 0-8057-9739-4 (alk. paper) 10 9 8 7 6 5 4 3 2 1
ISBN 0-8057-9740-8 (pbk.:alk paper) 10 9 8 7 6 5 4 3 2
First published 1990

To Susan, Mara, Alene, and Elena

Contents

About the Author

Larry E. Sullivan received his Ph.D. in history from The Johns Hopkins University in 1975. After teaching American and European history at various colleges, he became the librarian of the Maryland State Penitentiary in 1977. Subsequently he was the librarian of the Maryland and New-York Historical societies. From 1984 to 1989, he was professor and chief librarian at Lehman College of the City University of New York. He is currently chief of the Rare Book and Special Collections Division of the Library of Congress. He is the author and editor of numerous works in the fields of European and American history, bibliography, art history, and librarianship.

Preface

My research on prison reform began in 1977, when I was working as the librarian in the Maryland State Penitentiary, a maximum security institution, the second-oldest prison still in use in the United States. My work brought me into contact with all aspects of prison life—treatment, custody, and the attitudes of convicts and guards as well as of counselors, wardens, and others.

During my tenure, "treatment" and "rehabilitation" were still the official policy of the Maryland Division of Correction. I therefore received a thorough grounding in the methods of rehabilitation and their stormy relationship vis-à-vis the methods of the more custodial-oriented schools of thought. Trained as an historian, I became interested in the history of the way we treat convicted offenders in the United States. Most writings on prisons, both then and now, are sociologically oriented; that is, they probe the procedures and processes of incarceration with the aim of seeing what "works" and what does not. Most criminologists and penologists are problem solvers; they have an interest in finding a solution to the "prison problem."

The more I saw and researched, the more I became convinced that there is no ultimate solution to a problem that is grounded in the contradictory aims of punishment, rehabilitation, and deterrence. My interest was and is to illustrate how and why we got into such a situation; I focus primarily on the history of the thought processes that led to instituting and implementing prison programs and the hegemonic classes and ideologies in penology and criminal justice that dictated the methods used.

It became obvious after I began my research that few—if any—methods of rehabilitation or deterrence work. More and more people are being convicted of crimes, even as the United States continues in its "law and order" mentality. After a century of rehabilitation, the recidivism rate is higher than ever, and the prison's place in society looms larger than ever. According to recent statistics, one out of every forty-eight people in the United States will do time in a state prison during his or her lifetime, and among minorities the figure is even higher; for instance, one out of every seven black males will serve a prison sentence. Obviously we are dealing with a major social institution that affects large numbers of people. Our punitive control system may touch more people than any other institution in the United States, with the exception of the school system.

This book is thus not a hopeful or optimistic one. As long as we have social enemies, we will punish them and put them in prisons. It is unrealistic to presume that a radical restructuring of society will put an end to prisons as we know them. It is too easy to say—even if one agrees— that revolution will solve the problem, even as hundreds of thousands of people are currently incarcerated. The solution of ridding the world of prisons and deviant behavior is best left to the utopian-minded, not to realists. I have written this book as an historian, to delineate and explain the misplacement of the historical objectives and aims of prisons. Perhaps if there is a practical solution, it is the realization that the prison's primary mission is to punish and not to ameliorate behavior. Once that aim is understood, punishment can be carried out in a humane and dignified manner, and we can say that the penitentiary's existence is justified. My work will succeed if I bring a better understanding of the system that controls so much of our lives and of the reasons for its present condition.

I am especially grateful to series editor Irwin Sanders for his helpful advice and encouragement and for giving me the opportunity to make my ideas on social control known. Twayne editor Athenaide Dallett's useful suggestions made this a much better book and more accessible to the general public. One could not ask for two better editors. I, of course, take all responsibility for the content of the book.

I also want to thank several others who have contributed to this work. My former colleagues at The New York-Historical Society, Katherine Richards, Janice Matthiesen, and Helena Zinkham, provided research materials and aid during the initial stages of this book. I am very grateful to Phyllis Schultze, librarian of the National Council on Crime and Delinquency Collection at Rutgers University, who made that collection easily accessible during my research. My friend and colleague Susan Acampora read the entire manuscript, offered helpful advice, and was a constant source of encouragement throughout the project. Mary Q. Hawkes and

Dan Rubey read the manuscript and made insightful suggestions, for which I am grateful. I also appreciate the support and information given by my friend Brenda Vogel, who got me started in the prison field. I am grateful for the grant from the George N. Shuster Fund, administered by Lehman College of the City University of New York, which aided me in the preparation of this manuscript.

Finally, I would like to thank my wife, Susan, for being the best editor one could wish for, for making the time available during her busy schedule to let me write this book, and especially for her constant support and encouragement, which made the completion of the work possible.

Larry E. Sullivan

Lehman College, the City University of New York

Chapter One

Prison Reform from its Origins to 1890

"Sin No More"[1]

Prison reform has had a long and unhappy history that is more than the history of a movement and an institution; it is the history of such fundamental human problems as the nature of evil, sin, guilt, redemption, and expiation. The very ideas of criminality and punishment, when not buried within the dark and often mundane shadows of bureaucracy, provoke strong emotions and reactions.[2]

Imprisonment is essentially a ritual for redeeming sin through punishment, and its rhetoric often takes on a decidedly theological cast. The penal system originated in religious rites in primitive societies, when the collective violence performed on sacrificial surrogate victims was eliminated and systems of justice were established to protect the community. As an integral part of justice, the prison rationalizes revenge through retribution and isolates it in accordance with social demands.[3] Reactions to these social demands have historically structured the nature of punishment. This history is important, for as Dostoyevski once remarked, the way a society treats its prisoners characterizes the level of its civilization. Throughout the modern history of the penitentiary—and even its name reflects the religious category of penance—we see three contradictory goals: deterrence, rehabilitation, and punishment or revenge. Herein lies the built-in failure of the prison system. All these goals, but especially the first two, are unmeasurable. Punishment—the revenge ritual—is the actual goal of the penal system; but reformers have continuously deceived themselves with the goals of deterrence and rehabilitation. They have attempted to ameliorate or cleanse society by reforming its deviants; and since the late eighteenth century, the primary method

1

of reform has been imprisonment. This delusion is the double bind of prison history: Custody is incompatible with real rehabilitation. Effective changes in character do not and cannot occur in an artificial environment without almost total behavior-control methods. Without even mentioning the tremendous cost of behavior-control techniques, do we, who claim to live in a relatively "free" society, wish to control the minds of citizens to such an extent however deviant they are? If history teaches us anything, it is that social and behavior-control experiments have by and large failed. We need only look at the Cultural Revolution in China and the genocidal practices of the Khmer Rouge regime in Cambodia to realize this.

On a smaller scale, most reformers have learned by now that the behavior patterns one learns in a cage teach one how to survive in a cage, not how to live fruitfully in society as a whole. Therein lies the contradiction of the prison, and the history of prison reform consists of variations on the belief that positive change can result from incarceration. A system based on this premise is doomed from the start. No matter how benevolent the reformers, eventually it becomes clear that most prisoners are no better off and are frequently worse off when they come out of a prison than when they go in.

Enlightenment Ideas on Punishment

This problematic of the prison did not arise in the West until the modern age. For over a thousand years, primary punishments for transgressions of social moral codes were simple: death, slavery, maiming, or the payment of fines. Britain and its American colonies punished hundreds of crimes with the death penalty. Confinement was simply a detaining period before trial or execution.[4] But beginning in the eighteenth century, optimistic ideas of progress and the improvement of mankind influenced the "new science" of penology. This "science" attempted to give a larger purpose to imprisonment: to eradicate evil human behavior and cleanse the soul of sin.

From the Enlightenment until the late twentieth century, the philosophy of utilitarianism was the ethic that dominated penal reform. According to utilitarian ethics, a good action is that which brings the greatest happiness to the greatest number of people. This school of ethical thought concentrated on the consequences of a person's actions rather than on his or her motives for those actions.

The most influential Enlightenment thinker on penal reform, the Italian Cesare Beccaria, posited in his *Essay on Crimes and Punishments* (1764) a rationalist humanitarian schema. Punishment should be prescribed according to the gravity of the offense, creating a hierarchy of penalties. Beccaria's hierarchy of penalties was intended to serve a useful end: the prevention of crime—that is, deterrence—not revenge. According to such views, deterrence is caused less by the severity of punishment than by the certainty of punishment. Later reformers such as John Howard in England popularized this theory and translated it into specific penal reforms. The theory became the driving force behind American penology, starting in the late eighteenth century.[5]

The opposite of utilitarian ethics is deontological ethics. The central tenet of deontological ethics is that moral obligations and duties are binding and necessary. The main proponent of this view was the critical idealist Immanuel Kant, who stated in his work *The Metaphysics of Morals* (1796):

Judicial punishment can never be imposed merely for the purpose of securing some extrinsic good, either of the criminal or of civil society; it must in all cases be imposed (and can only be imposed) because the individual upon whom it is inflicted has *committed an offence.* The penal law is a *categorical imperative;* and he is to be pitied who slinks through the tortuous maze of Utilitarianism, in search of some (opposing) good which may absolve him from punishment (or even, from the due measure of punishment) where Justice requires him to be punished.[6]

Before the late twentieth century, the neo-Kantian deontological view had only occasional vogue; but in the 1980s it became transformed into the "just deserts" view of incarceration.[7] In our generation, penology has shifted from utilitarianism (with its three categories of rehabilitation, deterrence, and punishment) to retribution, pure and simple, based on neo-Kantianism.

It is not difficult to understand how we have come to this extreme view. We have only to read accounts of prison riots and high rates of crime, drug addiction, and recidivism in our daily newspapers to realize that something has gone amiss and that rehabilitation has not deterred people from committing crimes. Perhaps the penitentiary was never an appropriate location for behavior modification in the first place. But the penitentiary, originally created in a spirit of benevolence and charity, has had a tragic history. A brief look at its early history will help explain the penitentiary's continuing failure.

The Early American Prison

Late eighteenth-century America was ready to receive the Enlightenment's utilitarian ideas on penology. After the Revolution and the constitutional period, many prominent upper-class citizens of the new republic found themselves politically obsolete. Accustomed to deference in the Colonial period, when they had held offices almost by right of birth, these men were now increasingly excluded from the political arena by an ever-widening suffrage. They retreated to voluntary benevolent associations as vehicles for influencing society and for changing it in their own image. They approached society as an organism, one that they could mold through education, discipline, hard work, temperance, and religion.

Many if not most of these citizens had similar backgrounds: they came from prominent families of mercantile wealth and were well educated, intensely religious, and of utilitarian beliefs; they had an overriding concern for moral improvement. During the early days of the republic, they formed loose networks in urban centers such as New York, Philadelphia, and Boston, to transform society by developing public schools, libraries, mechanics' institutes, and similar institutions for the betterment of humankind.[8] They also set out to transform society by saving men and women from vice and degradation. These early reformers did not consciously seek to *control* people, as some historians have asserted; rather, they desired only to uplift those who had fallen.[9] The philanthropists believed that the new penitentiaries that they were creating were benevolent institutions that would aid in reforming society.

Although many of these early philanthropists took a back seat to active politicians, they controlled newspapers and wielded other types of political power through their money and influence. They were in constant correspondence with each other and with men of a similar cast of mind in Europe—especially in England. New Yorker Thomas Eddy carried on a lifelong correspondence with English criminal justice theorist Patrick Colquhoun. Eddy was typical of the reformers: He was ardently religious, and he had both a missionary impulse and the time and wherewithal to carry out charitable enterprises.[10] Another New York reformer, John Pintard, was involved in almost every type of philanthropic activity in the city during the first thirty years of the nineteenth century, including prison reform and the establishment of libraries and theological seminaries, poverty programs, and the like. In 1817 he mentioned that he held eleven positions in a variety of groups and organizations.[11]

Eddy and Pintard were only two of numerous reformers in the late eighteenth and early nineteenth centuries, when the penitentiary was born. They were organizers and joiners, and their powerful networks influenced all aspects of society. Their cause was a conservative one. In some sense dispossessed by the social movement of the American Revolution, these self-styled missionaries of benevolence embarked on a crusade of their own: to restore the moral fabric of the earlier time. In advocating prison reform, they were seeking a restoration of their own moral order as the only course of improvement. (They were also part of the voluntarism movement, whose ideology marked reformers until the advent of the bureaucratic professional reformers of the late nineteenth century.)

The early reformers firmly believed in the significance of a criminal's free will and moral responsibility in committing crimes. Only later, with the rise of positivistic criminology in the late nineteenth century, did determinism fully emerge and supplant this belief.

Philadelphia Quakers were the earliest Americans to advocate prison reform. In 1682, William Penn prescribed confinement as a corrective for criminal offenders in the newly founded province of Pennsylvania. In his Great Law, Penn abolished all capital offenses except murder and ordered labor as a punishment for crime. On Penn's death in 1718, however, the government reinstated sanguinary laws, reauthorized corporal punishment, and increased the number of capital offenses to twelve.

In 1787 a group of Quakers and others founded the first prison reform group, the Philadelphia Society for Alleviating the Miseries of Public Prisons. It is noteworthy that this organization's goal was to reform prisons even before prisons existed in the modern sense of the word. In effect, its main purpose was to create a humanitarian penitentiary under the "obligations of benevolence."[12]

The group was formed as a popular reaction to the penal code of 1786. Drafted by William Bradford, this code had abolished capital punishment for all crimes except treason and murder and substituted punishment at hard labor. Although the code was reformist and was influenced by Beccaria, its immediate result was to organize convicts in road gangs to work in city streets. Dressed in identifiable garb and manacled to each other or to heavy cannonballs, the prisoners presented a public spectacle of suffering that was inconsistent with the new humanitarianism of the time. The ensuing outcry against this punishment pressured the legislature to impose a "new" technique for the reform of criminals: "Solitary confinement to hard labor and total abstinence from spiritous liquors will prove the means of reforming these unhappy creatures."[13]

Philadelphia's Walnut Street Jail was opened in 1790. Quaker officials at Walnut Street believed in humane treatment and labor as the road to reform. They established prison industries, provided health care and educational opportunities, and held religious services. For several years prison discipline prevented any serious uprisings or revolts. The jail instituted a rudimentary classification system for its prisoners in 1797. There were four classes of offenders: those sentenced to confinement only; the select class; the probationary class; and repeat felons. These categories, however, were not necessarily related to the seriousness of offense. Most of the prisoners were confined together in large rooms, about eighteen by twenty feet in size. For the most dangerous convicts, the jail had sixteen six-by-eight-foot solitary cells. In addition, Walnut Street provided separate compartments for women and debtors. It was in this segregation of prisoners that the jail made its great advance. (In the past, felons of all kinds, both male and female as well as debtors and vagrants, had all been crowded into common rooms under the most promiscuous conditions.)

Because the Walnut Street system appeared to be so successful, other states used it as a model for their prisons for thirty years. New York (1796 and 1816), Virginia (1800), Massachusetts (1804), Vermont (1808), Maryland, (1811), and New Hampshire (1812) all built prisons following the Walnut Street plan: most had solitary cells for dangerous felons, common night rooms for misdemeanants, and large rooms for congregate labor. Most of these states also adopted the penal laws of Pennsylvania.[14]

In retaining the old-fashioned common "night rooms," however, the officials at Walnut Street had sowed the seeds of destruction, for as the prison population increased (and history shows us that the number of convicts always increases in proportion to available space), more and more prisoners were placed in this room, where they spent most of their time. Criminal behavior begets criminal behavior, and in a very real sense the prison became a "school for crime." Thus, a fundamental contradiction of prison discipline was present from the beginning of the penitentiary system in the United States. Reformers and even politicians were not blind to this situation, but they allowed it to exist, as they have throughout prison history.[15]

In 1797, Newgate Prison of New York opened its doors, the first prison patterned on the Pennsylvania model. Quaker businessmen and philanthropist Thomas Eddy (who would later be called "the John Howard of America"), was the man behind early prison reform in New York. Eddy was the leading advocate of humane disciplinary methods and was the first American to call for separate cells for all prisoners.[16]

Pennsylvania's influence on Eddy was strong. Newgate Prison, built on the Hudson River at Greenwich Street, bore a strong resemblance to the Walnut Street Jail. It too had solitary cells for the worse felons and workshops behind the main prison. Eddy designed Newgate, however, for felons only, whereas Walnut Street held misdemeanants and played the traditional jail role of holding suspects.

In its physical structure, Eddy and his colleagues followed the Walnut Street model a little too closely. Although Eddy thought highly of John Howard's ideas concerning the segregation of prisoners at night, he and Newgate's board inexplicably ignored this advice and had fifty-four rooms constructed; each held eight prisoners, who were allowed to mingle freely at night. A few years later Eddy saw this error:

Had the rooms for prisoners been so constructed as to lodge but one person, the chance of corrupting each other would have been diminished, and escapes would have been more difficult. The prison need not, in that case, have been so strong or so expensive. Absolute reliance ought not to be placed on the strength of any prison. Nothing will probably prevent escapes but the unremitting vigilance of the keepers, and a strict watch day and night."[17]

Eddy, like many of his philanthropist colleagues, believed that criminals were depraved but capable of improvement. His mission as he saw it was to eradicate the evil found in humans through discipline, education, and religion. Criminals could be reformed, he thought, if they were subjected to the proper methods. At Newgate, he provided strict religious services and a school for convicts. He restricted punishment for rule-breakers to solitary confinement and forbade corporal punishment. He also advocated individualized treatment, and like Walnut Street, Newgate classified prisoners according to a simple fourfold scheme: hardened offenders; those capable of improvement; men and women; and offenders under the age of eighteen.[18]

Although Eddy's record at Newgate during its first years was commendable, a bloody riot and escape attempt in 1802 caused a sea change in his thinking. It clearly called into question the promiscuous living arrangements patterned on Walnut Street and convinced him that the design of the prison was totally wrong. Thereafter, he lobbied intensively for a new prison to be built on John Howard's plan: solitary confinement for all prisoners in the evening and congregate labor in strict silence during the daytime. Finally in 1819, New York authorized Auburn Prison, in the upstate Cayuga County town of Auburn. The system eventually came to be known as the Auburn model of prison discipline.

The contradictory situation of congregate living arrangements was chronic in Walnut Street as well as Newgate. Both were overcrowded, underfinanced, and often poorly administered. The Pennsylvania reformers also learned from the failures of Eddy's and their own experiments and went to the other extreme—the total solitary confinement system. This also led to failure. Walnut Street's overcrowding problems precipitated its demise, and it reverted to a jail in the 1820s; in 1835, when the county prison, Moyamensing, opened, Walnut Street's institutional life came to an end.[19] Despite its failure, and even though reformers like Eddy attempted to dissuade some officials (most notably a delegation from Massachusetts), other states continued to build prisons on the Walnut Street model.[20] Humanitarian movements aimed at the reform of criminal codes were under way, particularly in Ohio and Massachusetts. The work of the philanthropists was spreading, and an increasing number of states in the early nineteenth century substituted imprisonment for capital or corporal punishment. In most states, however, the local jail was still the primary place for offenders. Sanguinary laws remained in effect in numerous jurisdictions; in many places hangings, floggings, branding, and the pillory remained public.

Thomas Eddy learned early on what we are still learning today but refuse to come to terms with: that most prisoners do not belong in prison. In a prison environment, prisoners learn two types of self-defeating behavior: criminal and artificial, or how to survive in confinement and earn good time for early release. Other prison activity rarely serves a rehabilitative end but simply makes the time pass faster. As one convict stated in the 1820s, "No man ever learnt any mechanical business in prison, that he was capable of practising with credit, when liberated."[21]

When Eddy conducted an evaluation of Newgate convicts, he found that no more than one in ten required the security provided by the prison; the other nine could easily have functioned well in free society. But incarceration itself rendered those 90 percent unfit for profitable reentry to free society. Eddy concluded that reformers must treat the causes of crime—an idea that foreshadowed the scientific or medical model of later in the century.

The proliferation of prisons in the early nineteenth century and the concomitant increase in the number of prisoners resulted in the unbearable overcrowding of these institutions. Both Caleb Lownes, the prominent Philadelphia reformer who was the "inspector" (warden) of the Walnut Street Jail, and Thomas Eddy retired from their respective posts, concluding that more effective penal systems were needed.[22]

The humanitarian, religious, and benevolent impulses of the first prison reformers thus resulted in failure and chaos. Compounding the problem, cities grew rapidly in the years following the War of 1812, and these cities were faced with an increasing number of poor who lacked traditional agrarian family support systems. These poor mainly constituted the prison population. Social dislocation after the War of 1812 fueled a crime wave in the cities.[23]

These social and demographic pressures brought new faces and new responses to deal with crime and poverty. Many of the new generation of reformers viewed sloth and intemperance as the root causes of poverty, and poverty as leading to crime. The old philanthropists' methods and intellectualism gradually gave way to those of the new group, who stressed stern and rigid penal discipline to achieve moral reformation of criminals.

The Rival Prison Systems

After the failure of the first prison experiments in New York and Pennsylvania, reformers in both states attempted new patterns of prison discipline. Sterner, Calvinist types took over the moral-improvement societies founded earlier in the century. Like the Eddys and Pintards, they were conservative and wealthy, and they were also more zealous in pursuing a righteous moral order in what one historian has termed a "benevolent empire."[24]

The period of reform from the 1820s to the Civil War can be characterized as an era of moral terrorism. The new penitentiary was intended to be not a place of fellowship and good living (as outsiders frequently, even today, view prisons) but "a place of dread and terror." Middle-class philanthropists responded with forceful measures to the burgeoning urban populations of vice-ridden poor. The poor and the criminals became the scapegoats for what the moralists saw as an increasingly disordered society. More and more theorists attempted to find explanations for the origins of deviant behavior. Most of the explanations centered on free will and the culpability of the criminal. Many of the solutions emphasized stern discipline; routine, hard labor; and maximum order in the reforming of the deviant.[25] We can almost hear the prisoner saying with Kant, "*Ich sterbe für lauter Besserung*" ("I am dying from sheer improvement").[26]

New reformers in New York and Pennsylvania enthusiastically set out (albeit on different paths) to set right the moral universe by subjecting the social deviant to the discipline of well-ordered penal institutions.

When New York legislators authorized the construction of Auburn Prison, the deficiencies of the congregate system were not yet completely understood. Auburn began on the congregate model. But the authorities soon converted to total solitary confinement and had a block of single cells built in 1819. These solitary cells were small, and many prisoners became sick and insane in them. This contributed to the termination of the solitary-confinement experiment in 1822. From that date commenced the Auburn system: congregate labor in complete silence during the daytime and solitary confinement at night. The leading lights who advocated this system—the legislative committee consisting of Stephen Allen, Samuel L. Hopkins, and George Tibbits—were all stern moralists and disciplinarians. So were the people they put in charge of the new system of discipline—Warden Elam Lynds, his deputy John Cray, and Gershom Powers, who would later be warden. To Cray may be attributed the infamous Auburn method of discipline: downcast eyes, lockstep marching, absolute silence with no communication between prisoners, a supervised work program, and the unsparing use of the whip for even minor infractions. This new order reflected well Stephen Allen's comment, "The reformation of a confirmed villain, however desireable, is a forlorn hope."[27] Rehabilitation was secondary in early Auburn. Its methods were considered successful—not least financially, because it paid its own way with its labor program.

From 1826 to 1854, the major champion of this system was the puritan New Englander Louis Dwight. In 1826 Dwight founded the Boston Prison Discipline Society, an organization dedicated to prison reform; its membership was composed largely of Congregational and Baptist ministers. The society issued annual reports on the state of the country's prisons. Dwight believed in stern discipline and the inculcation of religious ideas in convicts. To him Auburn was the prison most likely to cultivate industrious habits in its charges. He described the prison in glowing terms:

It is not possible to describe the pleasure which we feel in contemplating this noble institution, after wading through the fraud, and the material and moral filth of many prisons. We regard it as a model worthy of the world's imitation. We do not mean that there is nothing in this institution which admits of improvement; for there have been a few cases of unjustifiable severity in punishments; but upon the whole, the institution is immensely elevated above the old penitentiaries.[28]

But even Dwight could recognize the cruel brutality of Warden Lynds. The latter's reputation was such that in 1825 the authorities transferred him to Ossining, where he was put in charge of building a new prison. Using a hundred Auburn convicts, he built in three years what was first known as Mount Pleasant and later as Sing Sing. Sing Sing strictly followed the Auburn model of prison discipline.

Dwight and his group assiduously promoted the Auburn system during the first ten years of the society's existence. He was able to convince several states to build penitentiaries on this model. The first and probably the best run of these institutions was in Wethersfield, Connecticut; it replaced an old copper mine that had been used to confine convicts.[29] Dwight went on to achieve a measure of success in Massachusetts, New Hampshire, Vermont, Maryland, Kentucky, Ohio, and Tennessee.[30]

In Pennsylvania, after the failure of Walnut Street, the legislative acts of 1818 and 1821 provided for the erection of the Western (Pittsburgh) and Eastern (Philadelphia) state penitentiaries. The driving force behind this legislation was the Philadelphia Society for Alleviating the Miseries of Public Prisons. Imbued both with the Quaker belief that solitary reflection cleanses the soul and with the knowledge of the deplorable congregate conditions at Walnut Street, the society convinced officials to build both of the new penitentiaries with solitary cells. Construction of the Pittsburgh prison was a miserable failure, but the Eastern State (or Cherry Hill) Penitentiary opened its doors in 1829 and provided for solitary confinement at hard labor.

But the solitary-confinement system was a drain on the treasury. Built at the tremendous cost of $2,000 per prisoner (contrasted with Wethersfield's $258), the Philadelphia prison almost immediately generated criticism in a fiscally minded public. Auburn-type prisons were less expensive to run, and the use of congregate labor made them cost effective—even profitable. The Auburn system could run a prison like an efficient factory while also serving its primary purpose of removing threatening individuals from middle-class society.

The battle between the two prison systems—Auburn and Philadelphia—raged from the 1820s until the outbreak of the Civil War. On the side of the Auburn model stood reformers Mathew Carey, Louis Dwight, Francis Wayland, Amos Pillsbury, De Witt Clinton, and Gershom Powers. The advocates of the solitary-confinement system included Samuel Gridley Howe, Dorothea Dix, Francis Lieber, Roberts Vaux, Edward Livingston, and Richard Vaux.[31]

Throughout this early period, many reformers concentrated on reordering prison architecture: both physical space and interior, or spiritual, space. Every moment of the convict's day was arranged and accounted for; no choice was left to the individual. Prison architecture embodied the moral terrorism of the punishment; everything in the prison was designed to remind the convict of the wages of sin. An English encyclopedia article stated this concept well:

> The style of architecture of a prison is a matter of no slight importance. It offers an effectual point of abhorrence. Persons, in general, refer their horror of a prison to an instinctive feeling rather than to any accurate knowledge of the privations or inflictions therein endured. And whoever remarks the forcible operations of such antipathies in the vulgar, will not neglect any means however minute, of directing them to a good purpose. The exterior of a prison should, therefore, be formed in the heavy sombre style, which most forcibly impresses the spectator with gloom and terror.[32]

Most American prisons adopted Auburn's architectural style as well as its discipline; they were intimately entwined. The Auburn/Sing Sing–type prison consisted of a central office building that also housed mess halls and chapel, connected to multitiered cell blocks. The tiny cells were built inside, back to back, usually in five tiers; light was provided by windows in an outer wall separated from the cells by a corridor. On the prison grounds were shops or factories, hospital facilities, and a power plant.[33] Today the essentials of this plan remain in the majority, and in all but the newest, of American prisons.

The contrasting Pennsylvania architectural system was, as stated above, much more costly to build and to operate. English architect John Haviland designed the solitary-confinement model at Cherry Hill in Philadelphia in the early 1820s, and the prison opened in 1829. Its style was radial, with seven wings connected to a central rotunda that housed offices, a chapel, a kitchen, and other necessary facilities. The wings contained spacious cells that had hot-water heating and toilet facilities. Cells on the first floor had individual exercise yards. The Philadelphia prisoner stayed in his cell for the entire length of his sentence rather than joining others in the prison factory for group labor, as the Auburn convict did. In the 1830s, Haviland also designed the New Pittsburgh penitentiary and the Trenton, New Jersey, prison.

Haviland's design had little influence in the United States, but it became the prototype for prisons in the rest of the world.[34] It lost out in the United States partly because of the relentless opposition of Louis Dwight and the Boston Prison Discipline Society and partly because of accusations (which were basically accurate) that total solitary confinement induces insanity rather than penitence. More important, however, the Auburn model was less expensive to build, and its factories resulted in higher productivity in the prison and profits for the state. Among almost all reformers, a primary criterion for prison success was profitability. Philadelphia's solitary in-cell labor system limited the type of work a convict could do, and hence the costs of confinement were extremely high.

In the burgeoning laissez-faire capitalist economy of the day, the idea that a prison should be self-supporting was extremely persuasive. In an atmosphere charged with lust for profits, only a pretense of rehabilitation remained. Most prisons on the Auburn model were nothing more than factories that used the lower classes as enforced labor. As early as 1825, Joel Scott offered to pay the state of Kentucky a thousand dollars per year for the labor of its convicts for five years. He even constructed the prison, with state funds, and ran it prosperously until his retirement in 1832. (This was the beginning of the lease system, which flourished especially in southern and western prisons and is now being resurrected in the 1980s under the term "private prisons.") Many states were only too happy to turn over responsibility for prisoners to whomever would pay the price. Some states even paid contractors to take on the responsibility.[35]

The labor method used primarily in the North was the contract system, in which convicts remained under state authority but their labor was sold to the highest bidder. Both the contract system and the lease system were used in some form until the early twentieth century, when labor unions pressured both federal and local governments to pass laws restricting prison labor. Only the opposition of free workers to the competition of convict labor ultimately put an end to prison industries. It was then that prisons turned wholly to the state-use labor system.

This period also witnessed the further development of a system of classification of prisoners. Throughout the first half of the nineteenth century, local jails were cesspools of vice, filth, and vermin, controlled by corrupt local politicians. Because jails were used primarily as places to hold suspected offenders, little thought was given to segregating prisoners according to offense, sex, age, or other factors. Consequently, all sorts of people, including the insane, juveniles, and misdemeanants, were thrown together in common areas. The campaign against congregate living conditions was ongoing, and the idea that hardened criminals corrupted less dangerous offenders in prisons was current; calls were

also heard for reform in local jails. This situation began to change in the
1840s, thanks to the tireless campaign of Dorothea Dix, who criss-
crossed the country visiting local institutions. Dix was able to cause the
removal of the insane from jails and even from prisons and to place them
in separate mental institutions.[36]

This period also saw a movement to separate juvenile from adult offenders. New York State established the first juvenile House of Refuge
in 1825. By the 1840s, several other states had accepted the responsibility for the welfare of juveniles. Not only did they found reform schools,
they simultaneously crusaded for public schools for the education of all
children.[37]

One group of people who were confined primarily to local jails was
debtors. The idea that someone could be imprisoned for debt and was
therefore unable to work to pay off the obligation became intolerable to
the public. Beginning in the 1820s and gaining considerable momentum
during the depression of the late 1830s, a multitude of reformers and
labor leaders waged a battle against imprisonment for debt. Kentucky
abolished its debt law in 1821; New York did the same in 1831. Most
states followed suit by the 1850s. Other minor offenders were accom-
modated by new varieties of the House of Correction. Based on the principle of hard labor, reformers in the 1840s established workhouses in
Cincinnati, Detroit, Buffalo, Philadelphia, and other cities. Confining only
petty criminals, these institutions lacked the rigid regimens of the penitentiary system. The Detroit house, in fact, became a model for reformers in later decades.[38]

In the 1840s, the move to classify and segregate criminals also affected
women. In the early nineteenth century, women convicts had been kept
in large congregate rooms with little if any gender separation. In penitentiaries, women prisoners were usually placed in quarters within the
men's prison. For example, at Auburn women were confined to a third-
floor attic above the prison's kitchen. Rarely did these convicts have their
own matrons or any of the facilities, few as they were, afforded the men.
Exceptions existed; Baltimore's prison had a female matron as early as
1822. But in most prisons women had little guidance and suffered from
deplorable conditions.[39] They were subjected to rape, forced prostitution, and other brutalities. Most reformers neglected women because
they constituted only a small proportion of the overall convict population.
In the 1830s, one reformer found only ninety-seven women in the prisons
of seven populous states, and in the 1840s Dorothea Dix counted only
167.[40]

A significant advance in the treatment of women prisoners came in 1839 with the establishment of a separate prison for women at Sing Sing. Although the staff of the men's prison administered the female quarters, the women had their own matrons and a work program that included button making, hat trimming, and sewing clothes for the male prisoners. The prison also had one of the first prison nurseries in the country. The most innovative period for this institution was the tenure of matron Eliza Farnham from 1844 to 1847. Farnham allowed the women brief periods of conversation, visitors, music, and other amenities denied to the men. A believer in phrenology, the pseudoscience that claimed to discover a person's character from the shape and protuberances of the skull, she introduced phrenological literature to the convicts as well as other reading material that included novels (although some were bowdlerized).[41]

This introduction of "immoral literature" into the library, which was under the charge of chaplain John Luckey, caused Farnham's downfall. Luckey and a new set of administrators objected to the matron's interference and forced her resignation. Thereafter the prison reinstated a modified Auburn regime of discipline for women as well as for men. Farnham was a radical anomaly; the women's prison, like the men's, remained primarily a custodial warehouse to keep felons off of the streets. The separate women's prison at Sing Sing was the only one of its kind until 1870.[42]

Antebellum reform activity culminated in the founding in 1844 of the New York Prison Association (NYPA). Led by the usual blend of humanitarian merchants, lawyers, and other professionals, these middle-class reformers were imbued with a brand of romantic perfectionism that rejected the stern Calvinism of Elam Lynds, Louis Dwight, and the Boston Prison Discipline Society.[43] The founders of the NYPA believed in the ultimate perfectibility of humans and acted accordingly. Repudiating the punishment methods of most prisons, the NYPA's first report expressed the desire to "aid the sincerely penitent in their attempts at reformation—to protect the accused and the friendless prisoners against the impositions too often practised upon them, and to infuse in the government of our prisons a greater effort at reformation. . . . the great agent which has been at work to produce these results has been the mild, the humane, and the just spirit."[44]

The NYPA officers were very concerned with finding the causes of crime, and they were supremely confident that if they were successful, they could reform and rehabilitate the criminal, who would thereafter "sin no more." With the proper remedies, penitentiaries needed no longer be places of dread and terror. Instead of mere custodial treatment they used more humane methods.

By the early 1860s, the optimism of the NYPA had waned somewhat as its leaders realized the difficulty of rehabilitation within the prison setting. Its major efforts then went toward helping ex-convicts find jobs in order to assimilate them into free society.[45] The old prison disciplinarians—who, it must be emphasized, were still active—cared little for the ex-convict; the NYPA emphasized the outside environment of the criminal and ex-offender. In doing so, they laid the foundation for the parole systems and the prison treatment programs of the later nineteenth century.

Significantly, the NYPA's investigation of the causes of crime in the convict's family background, education, habits (extensive use of alcohol and other vices), and the like suggested the culpability of environment in criminal actions. This notion later led to one of the prevalent twentieth-century deterministic theories of crime that would largely supplant the older free will explanation. Most important, the methods of the NYPA led to the "scientific" and professional prison reformer, penologist, and bureaucrat who later would largely replace the antebellum volunteer philanthropist. The leaders of the association bridged the gap between the old and the new reformer.

The Emergence of the Professional Penologist

The post–Civil War period saw the emergence of a new breed of reformer, with a new mode of discourse. To be sure, reformers of the old order with their emphasis on sin and free will continued to be heard, sometimes at a high pitch; but they could not long resist the pressure of new ideas and methods.

Two trends characterized reform during the years from 1865 to 1890: the idea that if people studied their society scientifically, its inadequacies would soon disappear; and that professionals, not volunteers, should lead the way. The new reformers who brought this message (although they held on to religious rhetoric for some time) were far different from the old-time philanthropists. They were part of an emerging middle class of professionals—businessmen, social workers, scientists, and others. They regarded the breakneck speed of postwar industrialization and urbanization as causing the increased crime and poverty, and they were determined to use their professional knowledge and skills to order what they viewed as chaos. To achieve efficiency and rationality, these reformers applied new social-science expertise. Instead of voluntary organizations, they would build bureaucratic institutions staffed by middle-class professionals.[46]

To this new generation, knowledge was the key to social order, and social science the key to knowledge. It was at this time that a group of them founded the American Association for Promoting the Social Sciences (later renamed the American Social Science Association). The social sciences grew concomitantly with the natural sciences. They used the natural sciences' methods of classification to "scientifically" classify criminals. Also during this period there was a slow shift in thinking concerning the causes of crime: the idea that poverty springs from vice was transformed into the idea that vice springs from poverty. This transformation did not happen overnight, and there were countless varieties of environmental- and biological-deterministic views of the origins of crime. But the new bureaucratic reformers planted the seeds of twentieth-century Progressive environmentalism during this period.[47]

The reformers who best characterized the movement in the post–Civil War period were Enoch C. Wines and Zebulon Brockway. They were both outstanding representatives of the emerging professional who studies society in a "rational" and "scientific" way. Wines and Brockway were not necessarily more successful than their predecessors, but they did use qualitatively different methods.

Wines (1806–79) had been a failed schoolmaster and minister before he took up his life work of prison reform in 1862 as secretary of the New York Prison Association. Wines combined the rhetoric of the old-time philanthropist with the new beliefs of the social sciences. After his great success in raising money for the NYPA and expanding its programs, Wines set about inspecting New York's prisons. He found the conditions there deplorable, and he received the NYPA's authorization to make a nationwide survey of penal methods. With Theodore Dwight (later the first head of the Columbia Law School), he made a tour of all the prisons in the northern states. Wines and Dwight compiled seventy volumes of documentation and published the *Report on the Prisons and Reformatories of the United States and Canada* in 1867. The two reformers did not find a single prison that merited their unqualified praise. They did heartily recommend the so-called Irish system, devised by Sir Walter Crofton. The Irish system was a series of graded prisons or stages of prison experience, beginning with two years of solitary confinement and followed by a term of congregate labor that determined the date of release. A subsequent prerelease period allowed the convict to work at an outside job; then he would receive a "ticket of leave" or a monitored conditional release.[48] This system eventually evolved into the late-twentieth-century correctional practices of parole and indeterminate sentencing.

The report contributed to a movement for central control of penal institutions at the state level. At the time the report was published, local officials controlled most prisons and jails. Wines and Dwight spurred a slowly evolving trend toward centralizing responsibility in state boards of charities. The model for centralization was the Massachusetts Board of Charities, run by reformers Samuel Gridley Howe and Franklin Benjamin Sanborn. By 1869, Ohio, Pennsylvania, Rhode Island, and Illinois all had such boards. Frederick Wines, ably following in his father Enoch's footsteps, headed the Illinois board.

The prison reform movement gathered steam under Enoch Wines and his colleagues and culminated in the National Prison Congress held in Cincinnati in 1870. The new reformers attended in force and delivered prepared addresses. Wines summed up the proceedings in his report to the NYPA; he pointed to the bright future of positivistic reform and stated that the primary aim of punishment is the protection of society from criminals and that criminals—especially younger ones—can be reformed.[49]

But how was this rehabilitation to be accomplished? Wines posited the principle of progressive classification, "under which prisoners advanced from grade to grade, as they earn such promotion, gaining at each advance, increasing privilege and comfort."[50] Wines advocated rewarding good behavior and the practice of probation. He recommended more productive labor, education, and religion in the prisons. He was a firm believer in convict labor as an antidote for the vice of idleness. Successful rehabilitative methods, he stated, depended upon centralized authority rather than the haphazardness of local systems. And in a move toward the indeterminate sentence, Wines stated that the criminal should stay in prison until reformed. Significantly, he proclaimed the need to eliminate the political administration of prisons, which hitherto had been a bureaucracy for political hacks, and to place the management of prisons in the hands of professionals.

Most important, Wines praised the new "scientific study of crime" and declared enthusiastically (and not a little naïvely) that "crime . . . follows some fixed law. . . . Anyone familiar with this branch of the social sciences can predict with wonderful precision, how many crimes in a given year, and their general character. He can name the months in which there will be, respectively, an increase and decrease in the number of crimes, and will be able to foretell almost the hour of the day, in which certain classes of offences will be committed."[51] No statement better expresses the new faith in science as a means of social control.

The second important postwar reformer, Zebulon Brockway (1827–1920) came to prominence at the Cincinnati congress.[52] Hailing from an old New England family, Brockway had made a name for himself as head of the Albany County Almshouse, then at the Monroe County Penitentiary in Rochester, New York, and after 1861 at the new Detroit House of Correction (which Wines had singled out for special praise). Brockway's paper at the National Prison Congress, "The Ideal of a True Prison System for a State," set the tone for penal reform for the rest of the century. In his speech Brockway advocated classification of prisoners by age, sex, and offense. He would imprison incorrigibles for life, while others would be given a chance to reform. He believed that he could reform the criminal if given the proper tools. The primary instrument for this reform was the indeterminate sentence, centrally administered for all institutions within a jurisdiction. Or as Wines expressed it ten years later, "The true method is to place our prisons upon a proper basis, render the administration permanent, put the prisons in the hands of competent officers, make them really adult reformatories, and then say to the criminal on his commitment 'when you show yourself a reformed man, when you convince us by satisfactory evidence that it will be safe to let you be at large, you can go; but not before.'"[53]

Brockway's views were incorporated into the National Congress's statement of principles, which also stated that society should take responsibility for its criminals and their rehabilitation. They advocated reform through religion, education, industrious work habits, and the aid and supervision of convicts after discharge. Clearly the social sciences were now in the forefront of penology and reform.

The congress also advocated in these principles—without really understanding the consequences—relinquishing the court's responsibility and placing almost total power for the treatment of convicts in the hands of "professionals." It later became clear that the faith in professionals was somewhat misplaced. The indeterminate sentence ultimately worked against prison inmates; rehabilitation ultimately required conformity to the social order of the prison. Until the prisoner conformed, he would remain confined, at the mercy of the professionals.

Brockway tested his ideas at the new adult reformatory at Elmira, New York. New York had created Elmira Reformatory in 1877; the legislative act included the indeterminate sentence. (It also incorporated a maximum sentence, although Brockway preferred neither a maximum nor a minimum.) Elmira was limited to convicts ranging in age from sixteen to thirty.

Brockway set out to socialize the criminal there. He set up a complete regimen for them and incorporated educational, religious, and work programs. Elmira boasted one of the better prison libraries; it relaxed the silent system. Guest lecturers from the nearby college visited, and a revolutionary sports program was instituted, at a time when very few prisons allowed games of any kind. With its emphasis on total reform of the offender's character, sports became an important feature of prison life.

Also of utmost importance, Elmira emphasized productive labor. Brockway, like his colleagues, believed in the profitability of prisons, and he instituted several industries. (They flourished until antiprison-labor agitation later shut them down; afterward Elmira turned the workshops into trade schools.) Not the least of the industries was printing; Elmira's press was the first in a prison since 1800.[54]

Elmira pointed the way to twentieth-century reform. Penologists and reformers were laudatory of the Elmira model, and by the end of the century most new prisons were established and operated according to its pattern. Elmira's success helped revive the National Prison Congress, which had been moribund since the late 1870s. But many older prisons were slow to follow its methods.

The Prison Population

Who were the prisoners on which our reformers practiced their theories? Throughout the nineteenth century, a steady stream of the poor, immigrants, and blacks entered prisons, which were for the most part great factories for the exploitation of labor. As the century progressed, foreigners and blacks constituted more and more of the prison population. As early as 1826, one-third to one-sixth of the inmates were black, depending on the state, and 14 percent of all convicts were foreign born.[55]

As urbanization and industrialization progressed after the Civil War, immigration to the United States also increased. In the 1860s and early 1870s, 300,000 to 400,000 immigrants made their way to U.S. shores every year. From 1881 to 1884 alone, over 2.5 million came. In the second half of the century, about one in seven of the general population was foreign born.

The immigrants increasingly settled in cities whose habits and customs were strange to them; many had come from rural areas. They ended up impoverished and in crime-ridden slums. Their poverty and mores singled them out, and the societal consensus labeled them deviants. Later immigrants were more likely to come from southern and eastern Europe and Ireland than from northern Europe. Jacob Riis could state in *How the Other Half Lives* (1889) that "the great cities, which are our great crime centers, are also the great centers of our foreign population."[56] Enoch Wines declared even more bluntly that immigrant children in New York needed to be saved because "vast deposits of impure and vicious elements in the children of these immigrants from almost every quarter of the globe are thus accumulated at this port."[57]

By 1880, immigrants made up more than 25 percent of the prison population. Not only did they provide cheap sweat labor for the new capitalist enterprises, they accounted for the great increase in the prison population.

The treatment of the poor was even more blatantly inhumane in the South. Most southern states, although they dimly perceived the need for more humane treatment of prisoners, were still staunch advocates of the leasing system, of chain gangs, of Texas-style penal plantations. In effect, the southern penal system replaced slavery. In Enoch Wines's last study of American penitentiaries, he found that at least 75 percent of convicts in southern prisons were black. Before the Civil War, plantation owners and other private parties had meted out most "justice" and punishment for black slaves. After the war black offenders were turned over to government criminal justice systems, with the result that they were released from one form of bondage only to be placed in another.[58]

The situation was not much different in the far western states. A few prisons adopted reformatory penology, notably Colorado, Utah, and the Dakotas; but for the most part only a faint glimmer of the new techniques of the eastern reformers could be found in the West. Only in the twentieth century would California take the lead in correctional reform methodologies.[59]

Penal reform had evolved out of early-nineteenth-century volunteer philanthropy, which emphasized benevolence in the treatment of criminals. It passed through the moral terrorism of the Auburn and Philadelphia prisons to the incipient environmentalism of Elmira. In the 1890s, prison reform entered the Progressive era. No longer did most reformers believe that inner depravity causes vice and poverty; they now saw social conditions themselves as molding criminal behavior. This positivistic view brought new reform methods that aimed at rehabilitating the whole person, who could then reenter society as a healthy individual. Progressive reform concentrated on "health," following the medical model of the treatment of criminal behavior.

Chapter Two

The Age of Progressive Reform, 1890–1950

In the 1890s prison reform became part of the general reform movement known to history as Progressivism. Progressivism combined a number of trends that had emerged earlier in the century: the Christian fervor of the Social Gospel Movement; the rise of the new professional class; the use of scientific methodology in the social sciences; industrialism; and the tendency to depend upon government intervention to solve social problems.[1]

These developments resulted in part from growth of the cities in the early nineteenth century and the social dislocations associated with urbanism. By the late nineteenth century, large-scale industrialization had changed the character of the cities and consequently the country. The laissez-faire economic spirit had resulted in unbridled competition, low wages, and an increasing number of families and individuals reduced to poverty. Immigrants flocked to the cities to work in factories for little money. These newcomers brought foreign customs to urban life and thereby transformed the culture of the large cities.

As urban populations grew, poverty increased. By the turn of the century, the United States was no longer rural. New York City alone had 3.4 million people. Between 1870 and 1900, over eleven million immigrants came to the United States and most of them settled in the cities. The foreign population of the twelve largest urban centers in 1900 exceeded 60 percent, and in some of the very biggest cities, immigrants constituted over 80 percent of the inhabitants. As the newcomers came in, more and more of the native-born middle-class residents left for the nascent suburbs, which improvements in public transportation had made possible. The cities increasingly became the enclave of the poor and foreign-born.

As immigrants crowded into the cities, the urban environment deteriorated. In dilapidated tenements in urban slums, well known from the photographs of Jacob Riis and others, large families lived huddled into one or two rooms, forcing children and adolescents into the relative freedom—or abandon—of the streets. These were the days of boss rule in the cities, of urban riots, and of the first bloody strikes against the sordid working conditions and low wages of the industrial economy. Many social thinkers maintained that society was on the brink of disaster.

Reformers fervently believed that they had a mission to meet the challenges that social disorder presented to them. These Progressives formulated new ideas and solutions to social problems. The Social Darwinist idea that the individual is solely responsible for his actions and that government should not interfere with the natural order of things was giving way to environmental and biological explanations of behavior. The squalid conditions that industrial capitalism had spawned were all too evident. Society could not lay all blame for poverty and crime on individual free will or allow the poor to suffer and die as part of an alleged law of natural change. Society could not hold the individual wholly responsible for sinking into poverty and perhaps crime. Both poverty and criminality were partially products of the environment, and to eradicate them, reformers had to change society itself. Extraordinary measures were needed to create moral and social order. The depression of 1893–97 drove this point home with terrific force, when unemployment soared to over 20 percent; thousands of businesses went bankrupt. If any doubts lingered, the Great Depression beginning in 1929 erased them from the minds of all but the most reactionary diehards.

Contemporary historian Charles Beard characterized this period as a "counterreformation" that generated the first "war on poverty."[2]

Unrestricted competition and private property had produced a mass of poverty and wretchedness in the great cities which constituted a growing menace to society, and furnished themes for social orators. Social workers of every kind began the detailed analysis of the causes of specific cases of poverty and arrived at the conclusion that elaborate programs of "social legislation" were necessary to the elimination of a vast mass of undeserved poverty.

In an enthusiastic attempt to impose social order and good behavior, the reformers therefore embarked on a crusade to change the environment. The sheer massiveness of the problems put an effective end to the great voluntarist movements of the early nineteenth century. Social control was too important to leave to amateurs, however philanthropic they may be. The overwhelming problems of the nation created an awareness that only the government had the resources to resolve what the Progressives considered a deteriorating situation. Reformers now sought to effect change through government intervention.

The presidency of Theodore Roosevelt (1901–09) brought a governmental structure that would tackle the social dislocations of the nation.[3] Roosevelt created a professionally staffed administrative bureaucracy that transformed the nature of government; his public agencies were to intervene in social and economic affairs. On the local level, municipal reformers strove to make local government more businesslike so that it could undertake new social services.[4]

The reformers usually started out by defining a problem. Voluntarism was not dead, for they went on to form voluntary associations. Through these associations, they would gather statistics, analyze them according to the methodologies of the social sciences, formulate resolutions, and seek public approval for their solutions. They turned to the government only when direct action was needed. In the last stage, a public agency took over the problem and provided resources for the solution.

Many of these new reformers were driven by the evangelical moralism of the earlier era. The majority of Progressive reformers were middle-class Protestant, native-born Americans who believed in applying Christian precepts to social problems. They attempted to make Christianity relevant by helping the poor and downtrodden that industrial capitalism had displaced. In this sense they were truly descendants of the early-nineteenth-century philanthropists who had instituted the reform of institutions torn asunder by then-incipient urbanization. Moral fervor infused the Progressive reform movement with a similar Protestant spirit. The difference between the earlier and the later reformers, however, was that the objects of the new Christian benevolence were different; many were Catholic and Jewish immigrants who looked upon the reformers' ways as strange, just as the reformers themselves looked upon the immigrants' mores as repugnant.

Christianity gave the reform movement its spirit, but its methods were as new as the reformers themselves. They were not only middle class but were part of an emerging group of specialists and bureaucrats. In other words, they were professional experts who had chosen reform as a vocation, as opposed to amateur voluntarists. To these Progressives, industrialization had created a near-chaotic society; out of this chaos they felt driven to create order, even if it meant using coercive methods of social control. Believing that their expertise could solve society's problems, the reformers went about their tasks with the moral fervor of evangelists.

If spirit was evangelistic, the means were scientific. The new Progressive reformers had the self-image of impartial experts who gathered and analyzed data according to the methods of the social sciences. Once information was in hand, they made what they felt were objective decisions based only on hard facts. Such methodology resembled that used by researchers in the physical sciences; for social scientists—the new specialists in economics, history, sociology, and psychology—set out to discover the laws of human behavior in much the same way that physical scientists were discovering the unchanging laws of the universe. Most Progressive reformers believed that uncovering laws of human behavior would allow them to find solutions to social problems. But only the expert trained in this methodology was qualified to apply new-found treatments to the social order. The idea of the expert or professional that emerged during the Progressive period defined all future prison reform and rehabilitation efforts.

Concomitant with the rise of the social sciences and reinforcing the views of the new reformers was the increasing efficiency of medical practice and education in the early twentieth century. The germ theory of disease had led to discovery of the etiology of many dread infections; surgery made rapid strides; physicians became more professional; and with the rise of psychiatry, doctors took on new social roles in the treatment of mental illness. All these advances bolstered the idea that the individual is not totally responsible for his or her actions. The concept of illness began to replace the concept of free will as what determined antisocial behavior. The biological view of a "sick" society permitted the Progressive reformer to adopt a medical metaphor for its treatment.

The combination of the ideas of social control and environmentalism and the new prestige of medicine as a profession led to the so-called *medical* or *treatment model* of prison reform that dominated penology until the 1960s. The prison reforms of the Progressive era linger with us even today, and the history of twentieth-century prison reform is the history of the application of, support for, and reactions to Progressive efforts at controlling human behavior.

The fundamental idea behind Progressive or positivist reform theory was that human behavior conforms to general laws, whether environmental or biological. Behavior modification begins with understanding these laws. To Progressives, crime was a social or biological problem that could be treated both scientifically and humanely. But if crime is a product of natural causes, then punishment is counterproductive and barbarous. Penologists believed that the only way to make effective citizens out of prisoners was to treat the disease, not the symptom.

During this period, therefore, programs for the rehabilitation of prisoners gained support. Penologists experimented with a variety of programs and found what they thought was the correct answer to the crime problem. They treated the criminal both as an individual and as a product of his or her environment. Impartial experts gathered facts, analyzed them, diagnosed the problem, and then treated the offender on the basis of this information.

In effect, criminal justice was largely taken out of the hands of judges and prosecutors and given over to bureaucrats, psychiatrists, social workers, and professional penologists. In the words of two historians of Progressivism, "No Progressive trait has been more enduring than the tendency to entrust experts with social controls," in order to bring about change and to shape the future.[5] During this era, the three most prevalent techniques of the modern criminal justice system gained widespread support and became institutionalized: probation,[6] parole,[7] and the indeterminate sentence.

The idea of probation was first introduced into the United States in the 1840s by John Augustus of Massachusetts.[8] The practice spread slowly—in 1900 only six states had statutes governing probation. But probation became fashionable shortly after the turn of the century. By 1910 all northern states except New Hampshire had adopted probation, and by 1915 every western state had done so as well.[9]

What made probation so popular during this era, even causing a leading Progressive penologist to state that probation formed the basis of the "New Penology"?[10] The concept of supervised freedom in place of incarceration fit in well with the Progressives' philosophy of community improvement. As community based, it also accorded with the reformers' environmental concept of rehabilitation. To Progressives, probation for prisoners was analogous to the settlement house movement's treatment of poverty: it attempted to eradicate poverty by studying the living conditions of the impoverished person and by rectifying those conditions by providing personal intervention and counseling, procuring employment, and being a continuous presence with the client.[11]

It also gave professionals a chance to apply modern scientific casework

methods to individuals outside institutions. Some, like Thomas Mott
Osborne of Auburn and Sing Sing, attempted to use new methods on
those already in prison. But many Progressive reformers regarded working with prisoners in an artificial environment as inevitably a failure, and
in probation they saw their chance to try out new techniques and theories. They wanted to try the methods before prison life totally corrupted
offenders.

The State of New York passed its probation law in 1901. It allowed
police officers to become probation officers at their regular salaries, but
it did not provide for publicly funded professionals. Private citizens could
become probation officers only as volunteers. The University Settlement, under reformer James Reynolds, reacted immediately to the law,
charging that it allowed the corrupt police department to send out "experienced criminals" to monitor the activities of novice criminals. Reynolds believed that because settlement workers were involved in the
activities and living conditions of the neighborhood, they were the natural
choice to supervise offenders under the new probation law. Reynolds
was able to get one settlement resident to be named the first probation
officer under the 1901 law. Other settlement workers became active in
the practice on a volunteer basis; later the law was amended to allow
public funds to pay the salaries of all probation officers. [12]

Funding and administrative policies were primary causes of probation's
ineffectiveness during the first fifty years of its existence. Probation was
both managed and funded at the local level. Each locality set up its own
system, depending on its resources and its willingness to commit them
to the program. In general, most areas had too few probation officers
supervising many, far too many, offenders. This practice resulted in little
or no supervision at all. [13]

The state saved money through the use of probation rather than incarceration. It was much more costly to keep felons in state-financed
prisons than to release them on probation. But saving the high cost of
imprisonment meant little to the municipalities, because the latter were
now footing the whole bill and shared little in the state's windfall. Statistics on relative costs therefore are misleading. As late as 1943, penologists Harry Elmer Barnes and Negley Teeters praised probation as cost
effective and wrote that in New York the average yearly cost of probation
was $51.90 per felon, while keeping one prisoner in a penitentiary cost
$568.19, or ten times as much. [14] This was true enough, but the munici-
pality received no benefit from economizing for the sake of the state
government. (Barnes went on to write that in spite of this "success,"

too many judges still sent offenders to prison at the slightest provocation.)

The great variation among the states in the use of probation highlighted the arbitrary character of municipal control. For instance, in 1940 Rhode Island placed 60 percent of its convicted felons on probation, while Montana used the method only 14 percent of the time. Among the federal courts, probated criminals went from a high of 75 percent in the district court of middle Pennsylvania to a low of 5.8 percent in western Tennessee.[15] No set standards for probation existed.

From its inception to the present day, the popularity of probation has depended on the fact that it saves the states money. Judges have great discretion in granting probation, and they evidently enjoy this power. In order to economize on trial costs, as well as on the time and effort of a trial, the offender is often offered a plea-bargaining arrangement, in which the prosecutor reduces the offender's sentence in return for a plea of guilty. In effect, a guilty plea has become a prerequisite for a probationary sentence. The reasoning behind this is that by admitting guilt, the rehabilitation process has already begun. An offender who stands trial and is found guilty is by definition also a perjurer and therefore deserves a heavier sentence—meaning prison time. Most criminals are not fools; they realize that the odds for a lighter sentence are with them if they plead guilty. Probation usually worked—and still works—therefore, to wholly subvert the concept of fair justice.

The probation system is also run largely on a class basis. It is much more likely that an offender with a "good background" will receive probation than someone with a previous criminal record, someone from a family with a drunken father or mother, or the like. No matter what a judge's conscious attitude is, the physical appearance of the person standing before him does play a part in his decision. A probation decision can depend on whether a person can make bail and appear in court in a suit of clothes and clean shaven. A 1939 survey of judicial attitudes revealed that judges took a youthful age into consideration for leniency far more often than other factors.[16] This attitude flies in the face of other statistics that show that younger offenders (ages eighteen to twenty-five) commit many more crimes than their older counterparts. So probation from its inception has had grave built-in problems and contradictions and has had to face these problems throughout its unhappy history.

The Progressives also firmly believed that parole was a bulwark of advanced penology. Parole had first appeared in Alexander Maconochie's "ticket of leave" plan for convicts in the Australian penal colonies of the

1840s. Under this program the prisoner worked his way through various stages until he won release.[17] New England reformer Samuel Gridley Howe also advocated a form of parole in the 1840s, and Enoch Wines and Frederick Sanborn did so in the 1860s.

By 1869, most northern states had commutation laws for good behavior. These were an early form of parole, as well as of the indeterminate sentence. The indeterminate sentence was part of the reform movement that had culminated in the opening of Elmira Reformatory in 1877. The concept underpinning the indeterminate sentence was simple: The prisoner would not do a set amount of time for a crime but would stay in prison until reformed—with a maximum limit, of course. In Massachusetts an 1886 law provided for the indeterminate sentence and a grading system to determine the date of parole. By 1900, over twenty-five states had some form of parole and indeterminate sentencing structure in operation.

The Progressive penologists who advocated these measures saw them as providing release with supervision, not real freedom. "The granting of parole," they said, "is merely permission to a prisoner to serve a portion of his sentence outside the walls of the prison."[18] And, "Parole wisely and efficiently administered, guaranteed to the community that the released prisoner is a potential asset because of his institutional training."[19]

Parole and the indeterminate sentence were thus seen as part of a resocialization process, to prepare the inmate for returning to free society. The process of determining the success of the convict's reformation, again, fell to the professionals. As famed lawyer Clarence Darrow once remarked, in true positivistic Progressive fashion, "All prisons should be in the hands of experts, physicians, criminologists, and above all, the humane," and that sentences should be totally indeterminate.[20] And Socialist Eugene V. Debs stated that prisons should be controlled by objective experts who would "have absolute control, including the power of pardon, parole, and commutation."[21] It has been the support of the "correctional" crowd on one hand and the Progressive penologists on the other that has kept parole alive to this day. But from the beginning parole was unpopular with the public, which viewed the practice as "coddling" criminals.

Previously, judges set sentences according to predetermined measures relative to the gravity of the offense. When the indeterminate or minimum-maximum sentence came into effect, this decision was taken out of judges' hands. Although judges had the discretion to set minimum sentences, a convict's release from prison was usually now the responsibility of a parole board. For instance, if a judge set a sentence of from five years to life, the prisoner was eligible for parole at the minimum but could remain incarcerated well beyond that time. The main determinant of his release became his actions in prison, which were rated by prison professionals. Social workers, psychiatrists, psychologists, and classification officers examined, interviewed and scrutinized a convict's behavior throughout his or her prison career. When the convict finished the minimum sentence required by law, he came before the parole board, which determined his release date.

But who was on the parole board, and what standards did the members use to decide on release? The Progressives believed the boards should consist of professionals who had the expertise to determine how a convict would behave in free society. Their determination would be based on an in-depth study of the convict's personality characteristics, the degree of his rehabilitation, and the like.

In reality, however, parole boards rarely if ever worked that way. In Pennsylvania (which had one of the earliest parole systems, passing laws in 1909, 1911, 1917, and 1923 to govern its usage), the parole board at first consisted of the state penitentiaries' board of inspectors. Later on, it consisted of the state's lieutenant governor, secretary of the commonwealth, attorney general, and secretary of internal affairs. Other states had boards that were even more political. In Illinois, for instance, the governor appointed the seven members of the parole board. In practice, as University of Chicago president Robert Hutchins ironically noted, the governor usually chose a Protestant, a Mason, a Catholic, a Jew, a labor leader, a lawyer, a Pole—and one person who might have some expertise. [22] With such variations, it is easy to see that the parole system, like probation, was conducted according to no set standards and depended on the almost arbitrary whims of board members. In addition, parole boards had such overwhelming workloads that they could devote little time to individual cases. For example, in the 1920s a New York commission discovered that the state's board gave approximately five minutes to each case. [23]

In theory, a convict's release depended on his criminal history, his behavior during imprisonment, and his mental and physical attitudes—that is, the extent of his rehabilitation. The chief actors in making this determination were usually wardens and their staffs. Wardens were the greatest champions of the new system. [24] Before the mid-1920s, wardens held seats on many of the states' parole boards. After the emergence of parole bureaucracies that were independent of corrections departments, wardens were excluded from parole boards, but they still had great powers in release decisions. In practice, they had veto power and could prevent any inmate from being paroled by citing bad behavior or other violations of prison rules. The warden's power over parole kept peace within prisons, for parole kept hope of release alive even among convicts with the longest terms; if a warden could shatter those hopes, he and his designates had to be obeyed at all costs.

How did the parole boards determine with any accuracy the degree to which convicts had been "reformed"? Statistics revealed that almost 95 percent of prisoners, except those convicted of murder, were eventually released one way or another. Penologists therefore firmly believed that in the interests of society, they should—and could—make a scientific selection of prospective parolees through behavioral studies. A parole board considered a variety of evidence in its decision. For instance, it looked at the convict's record and perhaps felt that he had not been punished severely enough and therefore did not parole him. The board tried to foresee the future and determine whether he would commit new crimes. Then, as in probation decisions, it looked at external factors: family background, possibilities of employment, past employment record, and so on. The middle-class offender had a better chance of receiving parole than the lower-class offender. Repeat offenders had worse chances of parole than first offenders who had committed the same crime. And of course adjustment in prison was a prime determinant for early release. Since penologists thought they could prepare prospective parolees for reintroduction into the community through attitude adjustment, the convict had to behave and observe the rules of the institution. If he played the game correctly, he was returned to society.

The ex-offender would then be placed under the control of a parole agent. According to Progressive penology, "the crux of successful parole is supervision."[25] In their naïve faith in scientific methods, Progressives believed in successful parole predictions. They also believed that an ex-offender could be supervised by a professional parole officer who would be a "friend in need," who would have a proper caseload, and who would be paid a decent salary. According to 1939 recommended standards, a parole officer should have the following qualities:

1. Training and experience: College degree with a major in the social sciences or closely allied fields; at least two years successful full-time experience in social case work with a recognized social agency with extra credit for work with delinquents, or one year in a graduate school of social work and one year's experience in a recognized social agency.

2. Knowledge: (a) Demonstrated knowledge of approved case work principles, methods, and practices; (b) demonstrated knowledge of the principles of criminology and penology; (c) demonstrated knowledge of the elements of criminal law and court procedure.

3. Personal attributes: He must possess that quality of brotherly love that causes him never to lose hope for the reclamation of the offender. He must possess that patience and confidence in the ability of the individual, with use of spiritual and material resources at his disposal, to return the parolee to right living and orderly behavior. He must be in good physical condition, be of good character, possess emotional stability, tact, energy, mature judgment, and zealous interest in the work.[26]

But very few parole officers had these characteristics. Many were political appointees, part-time employees, or volunteers. In the late 1930s, only eight states had full-time professional parole officers who supposedly provided full oversight of paroled convicts. Even those relatively few professionals were defeated by the unwieldy system with its overwhelming caseloads. It was practically impossible for an officer to devote anywhere near the time needed for effective supervision. Nevertheless, advocates of the system persisted in their optimism and reaffirmed their commitment to parole at the National Parole Conference of 1939—although as one penologist stated, "Almost everywhere it is nothing but a palpable paper parole which neither provides supervision of these prisoners nor encouragement to reform."[27]

One reason parole has persisted into our era is the public perception that prisons are overcrowded. Whether statistically they are or not, legislatures, politicians, and others have operated on the assumption that prisons are overflowing with convicts. But building more prisons is a very expensive proposition. It is much easier to parole offenders than to raise the taxes necessary to erect new structures.

Many judges and police chiefs opposed the parole system as it was being practiced. Judges lost power to parole boards with the indeterminate sentence. Many judges tried to circumvent the system by setting almost equal minimums and maximums. (This practice was later abolished through legislation.) Police chiefs denounced "coddling" criminals by letting them out before their sentences expired. However, district attorneys were almost unanimously in favor of the indeterminate sentence and parole because they allowed them to clear dockets quickly through plea bargaining. And the district attorneys carried the day.

Perhaps the most vociferous opposition to the parole system came from the prisoners themselves. Statistically, the average prisoner suffered a longer sentence for his crime under the rehabilitative regime. It did not take prisoners long to realize that they spent more time in prison under indeterminate sentencing than they did under determinate sentencing. It was much better, offenders reasoned, to do time and get out sooner. Moreover, parole is not simply a rehabilitative, "humane" device; it is also a social control mechanism that allows the system to oversee the criminal's behavior not only in prison but for some time after release. Whether prison and parole were actually effective in rehabilitating criminals did not really matter; as long as a control mechanism—or the perception of one—existed—the power structure then retained its dominance. The prisoner, however, fared little better under the new Progressive regime. To him, control was still control, whether called treatment or some other euphemism, and life in prison remained grim and forlorn.

Behind the Walls during the Progressive Era

Progressive reformers succeeded in breaking down the disciplinary penal regime of the early nineteenth century. By the 1930s, most prisons had abandoned the old Auburn model of lockstep marching, striped uniforms, silence, and harsh punishment. To be sure, brutality still existed, especially in southern work camps and similar institutions elsewhere. But for the most part, prisons relaxed their discipline. Some even attempted innovative programs and methods. Perhaps the two most radical experiments were those of Thomas Mott Osborne and Katherine B. Davis.

Osborne was one of the first and best known of the new type of prison reformer.[28] He combined the evangelical zeal of an Enoch Wines with the investigative, "scientific" techniques of the new professionals. Beginning his public life as the mayor of Auburn, New York, Osborne read ex-convict Donald Lowrie's memoir *My Life in Prison*[29] and became firmly converted to the idea of prison reform. He was subsequently appointed chairman of the state's Prison Reform Commission and began a controversial career as a reformer. As a true Progressive, Osborne felt that he could not function adequately in his new post without experiencing prison life for himself. He decided to live with the convicts at Auburn for a week to get the feel of incarceration. Osborne's experience horrified him and caused him to view contemporary prison practice as unnatural and anything but rehabilitative. He chronicled his 1913 stay in his book *Within Prison Walls*,[30] in which he vividly described the prison regime as stultifying, brutal, and barbaric. He was convinced that nothing less than a complete overhaul of prison discipline was necessary. Earlier, in 1904, Osborne had addressed the National Prison Congress and proposed that convicts assume a certain amount of self-discipline and self-management within a prison. His experience within prison walls convinced him that this was indeed possible. His proposal for prison democracy fit in well with Progressive tenets already at work in the urban settlement houses, where immigrants were supposedly taught the democratic process. In 1914 he was ready to implement his plan at Auburn Prison.

Osborne created the Mutual Welfare League, whose objective was simple but almost revolutionary in the context of the old Auburn system. Osborne wanted to replicate the outside community as much as possible within the limits of confinement. This community-environmental approach would accustom prisoners to democracy. This was a radical idea. The principle was that discipline would be largely the job of inmate judges elected by their peers. Prison judicial decisions would be carried out by the free-world officers of the institution. Osborne defined the league as follows:

1. The League is a prison system not imposed arbitrarily by the prison authorities, but one which is desired and requested by the prisoners themselves.
2. There must be no attempt on the part of the prison administration to control the result of the League elections.
3. Membership in the League must be common to all prisoners; any other basis is false and will not attain the desired object—universal responsibility.
4. Under the League better discipline is secured because the prisoners will co-operate with the authorities when precious privileges are granted through the League.
5. Under the League all privileges are utilized as means of obtaining responsibility for the good conduct of the prison community.
6. The open courts of the League mean better conduct and fewer punishments.
7. The League has proved to be the most effective agent of stopping the drug traffic and combatting unnatural vice.
8. The League, when properly handled by the prison authorities, can largely increase the output of work and improve its quality.[31]

Osborne's plan was initially successful at Auburn, where the cooperation of officials and the public apparently greatly aided him. His success brought him the appointment as warden of Sing Sing, where he extended his community treatment model. Osborne intended not only to change prison discipline but to prepare convicts for reentry into free society, a hitherto elusive goal. Released inmates were expected to continue their self-discipline outside prison and to attempt to help other ex-convicts procure jobs and adjust to outside life. In other words, prisoners were to be resocialized and restored to a normal life *because* of their prison experience and not *in spite of* it. The league was to create good citizens out of convicts, not just well-behaved prisoners. Osborne had the best of intentions, and other Progressive penal reformers responded to his initiatives with great enthusiasm. Even Eugene Debs responded positively to Osborne's experiment and advocated its widespread adoption.

But the warden was naïve in his belief that his system would work in the long run. Osborne's system, although widely praised, did not hold up under criticism. No matter how much democracy jailers gave their charges, the latter were still restricted to the artificial confines of a penal colony. The notion of combining freedom and democracy was illusory and ultimately manipulative. Osborne and his followers did at least recognize the fact that a released convict had to work within a democratic, rather than an autocratic, prison environment if he was to adapt to society. But trying to do this in the face of political opposition, as well as with the contradiction inherent in the rehabilitative ideal itself, was Osborne's double-bind and became his downfall.

Primarily, Osborne ran afoul of the traditional custodial-minded officials, who viewed prisoner self-government as "coddling" convicts. The reformer came under fire from newspapers and eventually even his own superintendent of prisons. He was ultimately charged with a variety of malfeasances and indicted by a grand jury; only after a lengthy trial was he exonerated. By then, Osborne was burnt out and fed up, and he resigned his position.

Katherine B. Davis was also an exemplar of the Progressive professional.[32] She attended Vassar College and received her doctorate from the University of Chicago. If Osborne and his Mutual Welfare League typified the Progressive idea of community environmentalism, then Davis's experiment with women criminals at the New York State Reformatory for Women at Bedford Hills was an early and appropriate example of the use of the medical model in treating criminals. Davis and likeminded reformers emphasized the role of physicians, psychologists, and psychiatrists in classifying offenders. Those deemed incurable would receive life sentences, and others would enter treatment programs. Davis became head of the women's reformatory in 1900, and it immediately became one of the most active penal institutions in the country in experimenting with the medical model.

Davis was a proponent of the defective-delinquency theory of crime. This theory holds that feeblemindedness or subnormal intelligence is the root cause of crime. Defective-delinquent theorists also believed that promiscuity in women is closely correlated with criminality; many women were therefore incarcerated for sexual offenses, such as prostitution. In 1910, Davis received funding to study the psychology of female offenders who had what was termed the lowest grade of intelligence, with the aim of segregating them from those considered reformable. The following year, with the help of John D. Rockefeller, Jr., the Laboratory of Social Hygiene was set up at Bedford Hills to identify mentally deficient delinquents and sentence them to de facto life incarceration. One result of the laboratory's work was the defective-delinquent law, passed in 1920, which allowed for indeterminate sentences with parole and discharge decisions to be made by professionals at the reformatory.

With Katherine Davis and Bedford Hills, the medical model of treatment gained acceptance. In 1916 Sheldon Glueck, a reformer who was also financed by Rockefeller money, introduced clinical testing into Sing Sing. Glueck believed that one had to study the whole life history of the criminal before devising a therapeutic program for reform. He used a grading system for release under indeterminate sentence. Although many sociologists and psychiatrists attempted to follow Davis's and Glueck's lead, the general public did not widely accept the disease theory of crime and such programs were kept to a minimum. In 1931 the report of the U.S. National Commission on Law Observance and Enforcement remarked that the causes of crime were too complex to be explained by unitary theories.[33] Yet the medical and environmental models laid the groundwork for all subsequent treatment programs in penitentiaries to this day.

Except for the occasional experiment and the relaxation of the old nineteenth-century disciplinary regime, however, most prison life remained relentlessly grim, monotonous, and routine. Perhaps the most significant development during the Progressive era was the precipitous decline in convict employment. The lack of activities to fill the prisoner's time became a problem.

The nineteenth-century prison had had the goal of changing a criminal's character through prison discipline, which was to inculcate industrious work habits in the convict population. Both in the solitary Pennsylvania regime and in the congregate labor system of Auburn and Sing Sing, labor was an integral part of carceral community life. As early as 1822 a

Baltimore newspaper stated, "In carrying into effect our penitentiary system, much difficulty has always been experienced in finding suitable employment for the prisoners . . . but it is hoped that the . . . effects of the labor performed not only result to the advantage of the public, but the reformation and benefit of convicts."[34]

For much of the nineteenth century, many states operated on either the contract or the leasing system for labor. Under the contract system, convicts worked within prison walls, but their labor was sold or "contracted" to outside parties. Under the leasing system, the lessees actually maintained prisons and the prisoners for a sum paid to the state, usually after winning them at bid. Both methods worked on the profit motive (although proponents paid lip service to reform and rehabilitation). The states liked the arrangement, for they did not have to explain to voters the high cost of running prisons; the private business sector was delighted because it had the use of cheap labor. Most important, many state correctional systems could run at a profit because of these labor arrangements. Finally, hard labor kept the convicts busy and out of trouble.

The leasing of prisons and convicts was maintained throughout the nineteenth century in many states, including Texas, Mississippi, Louisiana, Georgia, Arkansas, and Tennessee. In 1894 Tennessee leased its whole prison population to the Tennessee Iron and Coal Railroad for a yearly payment of $100,000. When Wyoming became a state in 1890, it followed its neighbor Montana and leased out its prison. New Mexico Territory leased convicts to private business, and Arizona had a partial lease system. In 1885 thirteen states had private contracts for convicts to work in agriculture.

Although Alexis de Tocqueville stated in this classic treatise on penitentiaries that "no fear is entertained, that the establishment of manufactories in the prisons will injure the free working classes," contemporary workers' groups protested that prisons were able to sell products much more cheaply than their free competition because of lower labor costs. Protests against the noncompetitive character of prison industries became more and more widespread throughout the nineteenth century as workingmen gained strength in local politics. Eventually, state governments had to take action to mollify their constituencies and restrict the competition of prison labor.

Reformers, appalled at the brutality and other abuses of the contract and lease systems—which placed profit above the welfare of convicts—joined with free labor to abolish these systems.[35] The New York Prison

Association came out against contracting in 1870, and in 1888 that state forbade productive labor in prisons. New Jersey abolished contracts in the 1880s but then went to the piece-price system, which amounted to the same thing: The state controlled the labor of the convicts and then sold the products to outside bidders. In 1879, Pennsylvania passed the Muehlbronner Act that restricted prisoners from making more than a certain percentage of specific goods and/or from using power-operated machines to make any commodities that were made elsewhere in the state with free labor. By 1923, there were no more agricultural contracts, but 40 percent of all goods manufactured in prison were still made under the contract system and 60 percent of prison goods were sold on the open market.

In 1929 the federal government got into the act and passed the Hawes-Cooper Act, which banned the interstate shipment of prison-made goods. By 1932, only 16 percent of prisoners worked for private contractors. The Ashurst-Sumner Act of 1935 prohibited transportation companies from accepting prison-made goods for transportation into any state in violation of the laws of that state, and provided for the labeling of all packages containing prison products in interstate commerce. By 1940, every state had passed restrictive legislation prohibiting the sale of prison goods on the open market. Reform ideology and free labor had won the battle.

But it did so at a high cost. The most obvious effect of the decline of contract and lease was on prison budgets. Convict labor had produced profits for prisons, but by the end of the 1920s, almost all state prison systems were running large deficits. Prisons could find no viable alternatives to productive labor. The result was that by the 1930s, most convicts spent their time in idleness.

Progressives firmly believed that labor should be part of the rehabilitation process, and not used for profit or punishment. Under the old nineteenth-century discipline, for instance, treadmills had been established in prisons mainly to keep prisoners busy and to increase the horrors of imprisonment. Reform penologists, on the other hand, thought that the convict should work not only to retain order in the prison but also to prepare him for life outside the walls.

The only solution acceptable to both free labor and reform groups was the state-use system, under which prison-manufactured articles would be sold to state agencies and bureaus. In theory, the products would not be in competition with those of free manufacturers, and prison labor would supply the state with needed goods, such as furniture, stationery, and publications. To ensure the viability of this system, state purchase had been made mandatory in twenty-two states by 1940.

Unfortunately, the trades taught and used in prison were of little use upon release. As late as 1977, the state of Maryland, for instance, was still training inmates in the print shop on linotype machines, while free society was turning to computer-assisted printing. Convicts also made articles such as license plates that were monopolies of the state. The skills learned in their manufacture, too, were of little use outside of prison. In addition, many states, especially in the South, extensively used road gangs for public works. In sum, prison labor had little, if anything, to do with rehabilitation. The best that could be said for it was that it kept the prisoner busy.

The fact was, however, that the majority of prisoners did not work at all, even though in many states they were statutorily sentenced to "hard labor." Prison labor statistics are notoriously unreliable. Most figures in corrections department and prison reports were "cooked" to put the best possible face on their operations. It was estimated that in 1935–36 fully 60 percent of inmates nationwide were idle.[36] Other sources show that in 1940, under the best possible light, only sixteen states had more than 50 percent of their convicts employed.

One solution attempted was educational and vocational training programs. The 1939 *Survey of Release Procedures* stated:

No longer incidental to, but equal with industry at last, is training—not primarily because prison officials have come to realize that work is not a panacea for crime, but because they must conquer idleness at all costs or suffer from the mischief which it generates. Training—vocational, avocational, academic, recreational, social, religious—all are being made a part of the new program in addition to industry. The results may be more significant in the protection of society than the profits of prison industry have ever proved in the battle on crime.

Most educational programs in prison, however, were poorly run or nonexistent.

By the late 1920s, reformers recognized that the general state of prisons was horrendous and that once again they had to take measures to alleviate conditions. A rash of prison riots in Illinois, Colorado, Kansas, and New York drove the point forcefully home. A national commission was formed to study the situation and to remedy at least some of the ills found in penal institutions. In 1931 the National Commission on Law Observance and Enforcement, under George Wickersham, issued the report *Penal Institutions, Probation and Parole*. In well over 650 pages of data and reports, the Wickersham commission detailed the miserable state of the country's prisons. The commission noted the widespread idleness in almost all state prisons and the failure of almost every attempt to implement a prison factory system not dependent on contract labor. Wickersham and his colleagues described the arbitrary rules and punishments that were meted out in most prisons and the lack of meaningful programs for inmates. In good Progressive fashion, the commission devised formulas showing the cost of crime, the effects of immigration and unemployment on crime rates, and a host of other matters. It deplored what it considered the general state of lawlessness in society and the failure of rehabilitation in prison.

But the Wickersham commission did not give up hope. It declared that the main goal of prison was to protect society—but not just through custody. The only answer to the crime problem was to rehabilitate the criminal, and this behavior modification was to be effected in prison. To do this, the commission advocated the methods of scientific classification, segregation, providing meaningful jobs, and effective vocational and educational training. In other words, it offered the same solutions that had hitherto failed in practice.

The commission made some progress, however, in its suggestions for classification and segregation. The commission meant to classify inmates for treatment according to their crimes, personalities, and needs. For instance, it advocated the use of a penal farm for narcotics addicts, hospitals for defective delinquents, minimum security camps for minor offenders, and the like. It also strongly recommended segregating hardcore offenders from those considered prone to rehabilitation. Hence, it advocated greater institutional diversification for reform goals, along with segregation of types of prisoners.

Prisons throughout the Progressive period did attempt to categorize prisoners, but to little effect. After a criminal was classified, there was not much else to do with him but to place him in the prison to roam with the other convicts. Few effective rehabilitation programs existed. Nevertheless, the Wickersham commission came out strongly for rehabilitation in theory and against the law-and-order school, best exemplified by J. Edgar Hoover, who called reformers "the cream puff school of criminology whose daily efforts turn loose upon us the robber, the burglar, the arsonist, the killer, and the sex-degenerate."[37]

Ironically, despite the diatribes of Hoover and his ilk, it was the federal government that took the lead in implementing new prison methods in the 1930s. The Federal Bureau of Prisons under Sanford Bates attempted to institute a variety of new methods in that decade.[38] Early on, Bates set up a training school for prison officers, and with the aid of Austin MacCormick, he upgraded several educational, disciplinary, and industrial programs. Besides penal camps, Bates founded a medium security penitentiary at Lewisburg, Pennsylvania. Using architect Alfred Hopkins, who had built Walkill Prison in New York (called a prison without walls, because of its design), Bates had Lewisburg built on the "telephone-pole pattern," positioning cell blocks and other buildings so as to maximize segregation by type of offender. Bates also implemented a full-scale classification program under E. Lovell Bixby, who had made his name in New Jersey's classification process in the 1920s. Under Bixby, the federal system used classification programs to place convicts in maximum, medium, and minimum security prisons.

The federal government also took the lead in revamping the parole system. In 1930 it centralized the administration of all paroles; subsequently, the number of parolees increased significantly. That same year, the Probation Act was passed, which placed probation under regional rather than municipal coverage and supervision. Soon after, a few states saw the wisdom of semicentralization and followed the government's lead. Bates and his colleagues also recognized the importance of labor for prisoners. At their urging, the Federal Prison Industries corporation was formed. This corporation operated prison industries on a nonprofit basis, and other government agencies purchased the products. Several powerful congressmen opposed the operation, but in 1938 the corporation turned a modest profit, and opposition waned.

Many states followed the federal lead and implemented new classification, labor, and educational programs, with varying degrees of success and failure. Few realized, however, the inherent contradiction between incarcerating prisoners and rehabilitating them for reentry into society. The basic methods of incarceration were still custodial; convicts still learned behavior in a cage. Therefore little of what they learned, no matter what the program was, prepared them for a free and productive life outside the walls. No matter what innovations reformers introduced into prisons, convicts managed—as they always have—to use the processes for their own ends and to be resocialized and educated by other convicts.

This prison-acculturation process was first brought to the public attention by Donald Clemmer in his book *The Prison Community,* published in 1940.[39] Clemmer studied what we would today call different "interpretive communities" in prison and found that convicts went through a process he called prisonization, or prison acculturation, a defense mechanism that made them hostile to all prison programs. Other prominent sociologists, such as Edwin Sutherland, concurred with at least the idea of convict resistance and drew up new schemes to overcome it. But if Clemmer was right, and if prisoners naturally resisted treatment devices, the whole notion of rehabilitation was called into question. Rather than regard rehabilitation as a failure, however, many penologists simply tried to practice more efficient classification, to separate the hard core from those considered worth saving.

Despite the many efforts at prison reform, throughout the period more and more convicts were sent to prison. The situation became increasingly untenable after World War II, when the prison population exploded. No matter what new programs were instituted, they could not deal with overcrowding, idleness, poor food, and other conditions that prisoners considered deprivations. Reformers and corrections officials were faced with the prospect of building more prisons at great expense as well as with overhauling the entire disciplinary regime. As penologists pondered their dilemma, prisoners began to take matters into their own hands. Fed up with prison existence, convicts became increasingly violent. In the 1950s, the nation experienced widespread prison riots.

Chapter Three

Riot and Rebellion in the 1950s

Late on Saturday evening 29 March 1952, guards in the solitary-confinement block at Trenton Prison in New Jersey heard a convict groaning in a cell. Upon investigation, the prisoner said he was ill and requested hospitalization. Not believing he was really sick, the guards refused to move him from the cell. The inmate continued wailing and woke up the rest of the wing's population. The convicts demanded that their comrade be taken to the hospital and began shouting and smashing objects in their cells. The guards eventually took the complaining prisoner to the hospital (where the medical staff found him healthy), but the other convicts nonetheless went on a rampage and destroyed the furnishings in their cells. The administration withdrew the guards from the cell block, and prisoners ran free in the wing. The next day the riot ran out of steam on its own, and fifty-two convicts surrendered peacefully. Guards identified seven as definitely participating in the riot; they were sentenced to time in solitary confinement.

The trouble in New Jersey did not end on 30 March, however.[1] A little over two weeks later, on 15 April, sixty-nine prisoners in Trenton's print shop barricaded the doors and held hostage two guards and two shop instructors. After destroying the print shop, the rioters issued a list of demands. A committee of prison officials negotiated their demands and agreed that the "New Jersey State Prison would be investigated by an impartial, independent agency; that no corporal punishment would be inflicted on the rioters; and that an inmate committee would be formed for the presentation of grievances." Seventy-two hours after the riot began, the convicts surrendered.

The concession to form an advisory inmate grievance committee was a general demand of the time. It grew out of the limited democratic experience with Thomas Mott Osborne's Mutual Welfare League at Sing Sing, in which convicts had had a say in their own governance. At Trenton the administration allowed the formation of an inmate council, which consisted of elected inmates who would have, among other things,

the duty and responsibility . . . to ascertain the opinions and recommendations of the inmate body with respect to matters pertaining to the general welfare of the inmates and to faithfully and accurately convey these opinions and recommendations to the chief administrative officer of the prison.

Except in emergency, major changes in policy and practices affecting the welfare of the inmates shall be taken up first with the Inmate Council.

Every official in the institution will be instructed to cooperate to the full with the council.[2]

The subsequent history of Trenton's inmate council illustrates a major development in prisons of the period; the emergence of power conflicts between convicts and custodians. Although nothing in the council's mandate lessened the disciplinary powers of the administration—it was purely an advisory body—the administration viewed the council's responsibilities as encroaching on its prerogatives. They regarded even the appearance of official sanction of inmate power as potentially destabilizing for the formal prison power hierarchy, and the staff therefore resisted it. (As we shall see later, convicts wielded much power in the prisons of the period, but their power was in the informal prison culture, not in the formal prison system.) Thus, it was foreordained that what authority the council had would be abolished, and it was. When the administration denied several convict demands as intolerable, the prisoners held a sit-down strike, which gave the prison a reason to transfer the council chairman out of Trenton. After this action, the inmate council retained little significance in Trenton's life.

Contributing to the settlement at Trenton may have been the fact that the day before, on 17 April, over two hundred prisoners at the New Jersey State Prison Farm at Rahway seized several hostages and proceeded to stage a five-day riot. The Rahway uprising diverted media attention from Trenton; since publicity is always a major element in prison disturbances, lack of it tends to force convicts to give in more easily and agree to a solution.

Trenton and Rahway were but two of five riots that struck New Jersey prisons with hurricane force in the 1950s, and the decade became a period of major prison violence nationwide. Over the course of four years, more than fifty violent disturbances occurred in American prisons, ranging from major riots to escape attempts, self-mutilations, and sit-down strikes.

The prison at Jackson, Michigan, was the largest in the nation, with over six thousand prisoners. Although it was a relatively new institution, it was already seriously overcrowded in 1952. On 20 April of that year, one of the most famous riots of the era began there when several convicts took over cell block 15 with a number of hostages.[3] The administration's series of tactical blunders allowed to get out of hand an action that sound riot-control methods might have easily contained. Perhaps the most egregious error was the warden's decision to let the rest of the prison function as if nothing were happening. He released approximately sixteen hundred prisoners from their cells to the yard, where they almost immediately went on a rampage, looting and vandalizing the prison. The disorganized disturbance that began in the yard evolved into a full-scale riot:

Roving bands of convicts went into the great cellblocks and liberated the inmates locked there, smashing the brakes that unlocked whole galleries of cells at one time, shaking hands with the men they freed. They broke windows and ripped out toilet bowls, and the water cascaded down the tiers. In cellblock after cellblock the floor was ankle-deep in water, broken glass, and wreckage. They hauled mattresses out of the cells and piled them up and burned them, feeding the flames with guards' desks and clothing and documents. They fought with each other, settling old grudges. Wolfpacks of homosexuals prowled the cellblocks; an orgy began.[4]

Even more important, the yard rioters seized additional hostages for the insurrectionists in 15–block. By this point, the warden and his staff had become almost paralyzed and stayed away from the carnage. The administration's only course of action was to call in the state troopers, who then occupied the prison. It took most of a violent day to get the thousands of prisoners under control and back into their cells. Fifteen convicts had been wounded, and one killed. The warden wisely decided to feed the men in their cells that night rather than release them to the mess hall.

The state troopers did not, however, end the hostage situation in 15–block. By this time, two hardened convicts (some called them psychopaths) were in complete command, with twelve guards as hostages. They made definite demands of the administration. First, they wanted 15–block remodeled to include better facilities for hygiene, convenience, and treatment. They desired access to counselors and more competent personnel for treating mental cases. They complained of outmoded segregation policies and of the brutality of the guards, who, they charged, used illegal weapons such as rubber hoses and "wrist-breakers." They complained of poor dental and medical treatment and even lack of treatment. They insisted on no reprisals for participants in the uprising.

As at Trenton, they demanded the election of an inmate council that would meet with prison officials but that, unlike Trenton's, would also have the power to review and veto all rules and regulations pertaining to prisoners. During the negotiations, the convicts were persuaded that no prison would give prisoners veto power; they therefore changed the demand to the creation of an advisory council like the one at Trenton. Most significant, the convicts demanded that the parole board change its policies to give equal treatment to all convicts. Initially, the leaders had wanted the parole board and the indeterminate sentence abolished; later, they wanted fixed terms and automatic release—in effect, a reversion to the old penology and a signal failure for the ideas of Progressive penology.

After long negotiations, especially with criminologist and assistant warden for treatment Vernon Fox, the convicts accepted emendations and deletions to their demands and settled with the administration and the state's governor. At the behest of one of the riot leaders, Fox made a speech that in effect congratulated the insurrectionists as honorable men. This naïve political mistake eventually cost Fox his job and led to the repudiation of the administration's concessions to the convicts.

Following the Jackson and Trenton riots, 21–23 October 1952, convicts at Menard State Prison in Illinois rioted and held several officers hostage. The riot ended only when state troopers stormed the prison and physically stopped the rebellion. On the same day the Menard riot was ended, twelve hundred convicts at the Ohio State Penitentiary also rose in violence. The Ohio inmates took no hostages, but they literally took over the prison, burned several buildings, and caused millions of dollars in property damage. The uprising finally ended when the state guard came in and forced the convicts to surrender.

Also in October, three hundred convicts rioted in the new Utah Penitentiary, where they took guards as hostages, ransacked the commissary, and wrought havoc throughout the prison. In November, another smaller riot broke out at Jackson, and a minor uprising erupted in the New Mexico State Penitentiary.

In 1953, New Mexico prisoners rebelled again, as did convicts at the Western Penitentiary in Pennsylvania. Other prison disturbances during the years 1951–53 occurred in Soledad, California, Oregon, Minnesota, Washington, Massachusetts, and Colorado. Many prisoners protested their lot through self-mutilation. This period of extraordinary prison violence revealed a penal system that was on the brink of widespread disaster.

Although there were some disturbances in southern states, such as North Carolina and Georgia, most of the major riots took place in the northern and western parts of the country. In the South the prevailing system was the large penal farm, which resembled the antebellum slave plantation more than the fortress-type northern penitentiary. Consequently, it was almost as difficult to instigate a riot in southern prisons as it would have been on a plantation.

Rebellion at the penal farms therefore took other forms. In 1951, the Louisiana public received a shock from a scandal at the state penal farm at Angola. Thirty-seven convicts took razor blades and slashed their heel tendons. They took this desperate action to escape the brutality of their day-to-day existence and to protest what they considered deplorable conditions at the farm—poor food, brutal guards, lack of recreation, overwork in the fields, and the lack of treatment programs.[5] The following year, a national magazine characterized Angola as "America's worst prison."

Angola typified the southern prison system.[6] These institutions had very few professionals of any kind—including guards. Angola itself had only nineteen paid guards to watch approximately two thousand convicts. Most of the guards were convicts themselves and were frequently rewarded with parole for shooting prisoners attempting escape. The food was rotten and hygiene was almost nonexistent; convicts slept in muddy and filthy clothes for days on end and were allowed to wash only once a week. The limited classification system concentrated almost exclusively on the physical strength of the convict in order to place him in the proper job. Few if any treatment or vocational programs existed. The men worked from daylight to darkness on farms or roads, frequently shackled. At night they slept either in barracks or in mobile cages.

Although most of the southern states had a central penitentiary, the majority of the convicts were placed on the farms; only the incorrigible escapees were locked up in the large institutions. The primary objective of the southern system was to wring labor out of the convicts. Although the overwhelming brutality and oppression of this system precluded riots and insurrections, it did induce revolt through escape or self-mutilation, as at Angola.

What had happened to Progressive penology, that conditions at the prisons throughout the country were so atrocious? The major revolts occurred in many of the states where treatment and rehabilitation programs had been introduced. But some disturbance occurred in almost every state correctional system in the country. How could prison conditions have reached such a point after Progressive reform and rehabilitation? The professionals searched for answers.

In 1948, Federal Bureau of Prisons Director James V. Bennett summarized the problem concisely in his annual report.

Even our modern prison system is proceeding on a rather uncertain course because its administration is necessarily a series of compromises. On the one hand, prisons are expected to punish; on the other, they are supposed to reform. They are expected to discipline rigorously at the same time that they teach self-reliance. They are built to be operated like vast impersonal machines, yet they are expected to fit men to live normal community lives. They operate in accordance with a fixed autocratic routine, yet they are expected to develop individual initiative. All too frequently restrictive laws force prisoners into idleness despite the fact that one of their primary objectives is to teach men how to earn an honest living. They refuse the prisoner a voice in self-government, but they expect him to become a thinking citizen in a democratic society. To some, prisons are nothing but "country clubs" catering to the whims and fancy of the inmates. To others the prison atmosphere seems charged only with bitterness, rancor, and an all-pervading sense of defeat. And so the whole paradoxical scheme continues, because our ideas and views regarding the function of correctional institutions in our society are confused, fuzzy, and nebulous.[7]

Although penologists like Bennett could correctly define the problem, the solutions they came up with were confined to Progressive categories. They stated that the Progressive reforms had never been given a real chance to work. Vernon Fox was a firm believer in Progressive penology even after the riot that caused him to lose his job. In fact, he naively believed that his settlement of the Jackson riot was a model of Progressive penology. They could not shake the methods of the past or dismiss the hope for rehabilitation and behavior modification. It was difficult

for them to see the contradictions inherent in the carceral system
itself.

But they could not deny that the riots demonstrated the widespread
failure of rehabilitation and reform efforts as they had been practiced.
For the first time in many years, the media focused on prison conditions.
Scandal forced even the most reactionary politicians to pay some attention to their state penal institutions and alleviate at least some of the most
primitive conditions and pay lip service to reform. But first the professionals had to answer to the public for the failure of Progressive
penology.

In 1953, the American Prison Association appointed a commission to
study the causes of the wave of prison violence. Chaired by California's
correctional commissioner, Richard McGee, the commission included
Sanford Bates of New Jersey, James Bennett, Joseph Ragen of
Stateville Prison in Illinois, and the quintessential Progressive, Austin
MacCormick.

In its report, entitled *A Statement concerning Causes, Preventive Measures, and Methods of Controlling Prison Riots and Disturbances,* the
commission found that faulty prison administration had been the primary
cause of the riots.[8] According to the report, the underlying elements of
administrative failure were

  1. inadequate financial support and official public indifference;
  2. substandard personnel;
  3. enforced idleness;
  4. lack of professional leadership and professional programs;
  5. excessive size and overcrowding of institutions;
  6. political domination and motivation of management;
  7. unwise sentencing and parole practices.

The commission called for better-trained guards to replace the ill-trained
ones prone to brutality, more programs and work to replace the idleness
that produces unrest, and a better understanding between custody and
treatment factions. Furthermore, it recommended "classification aimed
at an individualized analytical study of each inmate; segregation of types
for purposes of better control, training and treatment, and to prevent
moral contamination; general education and vocational training; religious
training and worship; directed recreation programs; medical and psychi-

atric treatment; library services; social casework; release counseling; and varied employment activities. "[9]

The commission decried the large size of contemporary prisons; it thought any institution containing more than twelve hundred men unsafe. (Jackson contained more than six thousand.) It decried the politicization of the control of prisons, inequitable sentences, and poor parole practices. But the commission also argued that the faults in prisons were beyond the control of the administrators at that time. It called for strict discipline but also recognition of the legitimate grievances of prisoners and the establishment of inmate councils. Riotous uprisings, it maintained, began as spontaneous outbursts against specific conditions the convicts deemed intolerable—poor food, medical care, brutality, and the like. Interestingly, neither the convicts in their demands nor the professionals in their study challenged the generic carceral system itself. All took the existence of the prison system for granted and decried only poor administration and conditions within prisons that had been brought about by forces beyond the administrators' control.

Although they agreed with the commission about prison conditions, academic penologists thought the reasons for prison violence lay farther beneath the surface, and their theories focused on the social function of the prison population. Influential penologists who tackled the problem in this way were Gresham Sykes, Richard Korn, Lloyd McCorkle and Clarence Schrag. According to them, much of the violence in the prisons was caused by the acculturation process among the institutionalized. They focused on the function of prison social structure and culture, using Donald Clemmer's concept of prisonization.

This concept was revised and expanded upon by Clemmer himself, who as superintendent of prisons in Washington, D.C., became a much-sought-after prison consultant. In a 1950 article Clemmer reiterated his belief in what he called the "universal factors of prisonization."[10] He enumerated several so-called factors that lead to prisonization: convicts' unstable personalities and inadequate personal relations before commitment; their negative relations with people outside prison; long sentences; their willingness to participate in gambling and abnormal sex in prison; and their eager participation in the primary convict control group. Clemmer felt that these factors worked against rehabilitation efforts, even in prisons with what he termed "progressive" training or treatment programs. But Clemmer ended his article on an optimistic note, basically calling for better methods within the same tradition of the social sciences that heretofore had failed so miserably: "As humanitarianism increases and as the sciences which deal with human nature improve their techniques of treating the maladjusted, and as other better methods . . . are found to deal with violators of the law . . . the criminality of the offender, which is currently increased by the methods used, may well be decreased in that brave new world somewhere ahead."[11]

Four years later, Lloyd W. McCorkle and Richard Korn attempted to deal with the resocialization process by explaining in sociopsychological terms just what goes wrong when a criminal enters prison.[12] McCorkle and Korn analyzed the prison community as a functional social unit that consists of two distinct but interdependent social structures, one official and the other unofficial. The official structure is the administrative order, where power is arranged hierarchically, descending from the warden. The unofficial structure is the inmate social order. This structure is also hierarchical and extremely authoritarian. To make it in prison, the prisoner has to adapt to the prevalent codes. Those prisoners who do not and identify with free, noncriminal society instead are excluded and become social rejects within the walls.

The main function of the unofficial social structure, according to the authors, is adaptive—that is, it "protect[s] its members from the effects of internalizing social rejection." The antisocial acts of the criminal had caused him or her to experience social rejection in free society; these same acts provide group acceptance for the offender in prison. The convict adheres to certain practices and codes in prison in order to receive this protection and belong to the dominant group. These practices include keeping one's distance from the captors, the taboo on informing or "snitching," retaining a sense of dignity or autonomy in the face of the custodians, and the like.

The formal prison authorities, the custodians, make use of the inmate social structure to maintain order in the prison. But McCorkle and Korn asserted that they are more used than using. High-status members in the inmate social order use their authority to keep discipline among the ranks; in return they receive better job assignments and living quarters than low-status convicts or outsiders. The authorities in effect buy peace with the system.

McCorkle and Korn observed that efforts toward the "humane treatment" of convicts made by the rehabilitative movement had been failures. This failure occurred primarily because of the unofficial prison social structure.

The inmate social system appears to function as an adaptation to social rejection and punishment, enabling the offender to avoid the pathological effects of converting the hostility of society into hatred of himself. Rather than internalizing this hostility, as does the typical neurotic, the adaptive inmate appears to be able to turn it back upon society, using the misery of prison life as his reasonable pretext. If this interpretation is correct, it may help to explain the failure of any attempt to rehabilitate which is based on easing the harshness of prison life.

The prisonized inmate actually needs harsh conditions, the authors argued, because he needs something to protest. If conditions were alleviated, the convict would find something else to rail against. That is why, McCorkle and Korn stated, the "bleeding hearts" of prison reform have made matters worse by attempting to treat convicts humanely.

In attempting to offer solutions to the problem of prison acculturation, McCorkle and Korn's analysis breaks down and fades into vagueness. Group therapy is the ideal solution that they present, therapy carried out under a system of strict control. Yet they also found successful therapy impossible, within the actual context of large institutions with their propensity for prisonization. All they finally proposed was that new learning situations be created for the establishment of new patterns of behavior. To create these learning situations, professionals and custodians must work together and use the tools of scientific social analysis. It is obvious that the authors could not see beyond their own mental categories, falling back on the "sciences" and the old saw of working together.

Although they did not develop the idea in their paper, the two criminologists did see that disrupting the normal interaction between the formal authorities and the convict apparatus causes severe friction. In normal interaction, a balance is maintained. When a prisoner becomes part of the prison culture, "a major therapeutic objective of the prison experience, namely, that of learning compliance to duly constituted authority" is lost. The custodian, by favoring selected prison leaders who use these illegal favors as leverage, thereby compromises his authority and loses power and eventually overall control of the situation. At that point, violence is possible. Harmony may be restored only through capitulation or force. McCorkle and Korn did not apply this analysis to the riots of the period, but in a later work they noted that in many of the institutions that experienced riots during the 1950s, the most dangerous and aggressive convicts held the most strategic jobs, which confirmed their observations on the convict social system.[13]

Other penologists carried the theory a step further to explain the violent outbursts and the emergence of leadership within prison culture. Clarence Schrag, in his 1954 article "Leadership Among Prison Inmates,"[14] buttressed McCorkle and Korn's opposition to mingling different types of convicts within large institutions. He explained the failure of treatment and rehabilitation by emphasizing the unofficial prison social structure. In studying inmates in a western prison, Schrag found that the prisoners who became leaders were primarily those with "criminal maturity, comparatively permanent tenure in the institution, and habits of aggressiveness and violence." These convicts were the least likely to have positive attitudes toward free society and were therefore poor candidates for any type of treatment program. They were the most prone to accept and perpetuate prison culture as well as to rebel against incursions on the prevailing convict codes. Schrag found that the leaders had a high incidence of psychoneurosis and psychopathy.

Schrag concluded that violent recidivists would rise to the top of the prison social hierarchy through acts of violence or psychopathic behavior. The only way to prevent this was to segregate the violent from those who were potentially responsive to certain treatment programs. In other words, effective classification programs were necessary to thwart prison acculturation and violence. Ultimately, such segregation would prevent psychopaths (as the leaders of the Michigan riot were called) from staging insurrections. Other studies have confirmed the observation that leaders in prison communities are the ones who most resist resocialization.[15]

It becomes clear in these analyses of the riots that convicts rebelled because of what they considered abuses in the power structure of the prison system, not because of the prison system itself. In the postwar period, prisons in the North and West became bureaucratized and professionals took over many of the functions, such as handing out job and cell assignments, that convicts had previously held. (Because of the agricultural character of most southern prisons, this bureaucratization did not develop there until later; in fact, convict guards were used on some penal farms into the 1970s.) With this shift in control, some of the privileges of the convicts were revoked, and a degree of friction resulted that could be resolved only by revolt or by capitulation. Extremely oppressive conditions did not play a part in the riots; in fact, they sometimes prevented them (as we will see below in the case of Stateville) or channeled resentment into self-mutilation, as at Angola. The primary catalyst for a riot was an upset in the power equilibrium.

It was in this context in 1958 that Gresham Sykes studied the social structure of Trenton prison and linked the concept of inmate power with the outbreak of the riot there. [16] Sykes immediately recognized the contradictory nature of prevailing penal philosophy, composed of both reform and custody: "There is the question of the value or priority to be attached to the maintenance of order as opposed to possibly competing objectives. If extensive regulations . . . are used, prison officials are likely to run headlong into the supporters of reform who argue that such procedures are basically inimical to the doctor-patient relationship which should serve as the model for therapy." Sykes then went on to describe the ambiguities of changing criminals into noncriminals.

Formal prison power, Sykes agreed, is hierarchical and descends from the warden to the guard. The convicts, however, are under no moral obligation to obey this prison authority; unlike free society the legitimacy of authority is not recognized, and inmates feel no sense of duty to that authority. The prison social system is more like that of a conquered country, where a small occupying force controls a large indigenous population. As in a conquered country, the only way to enforce obedience is to coerce, cajole, and bully. But one can coerce only so much; the prison has to operate on a daily basis, and the guards cannot continuously beat the prisoners to march, eat, and work. Therefore, the controlled and the controllers work out a modus vivendi to keep order in the prison. This is where the inmate power structure comes into play.

In order to retain a modicum of control, Sykes argued, the keepers must informally sanction some illegal acts of the convicts. The guard is the authority who has the closest daily contact with the prisoners; to a large extent, he depends on the convict for his job, because he is rated largely on how well he keeps order among his charges; if he cannot handle them, his position is in danger. He will therefore frequently fail to report infractions, will neglect security requirements, or will transport contraband.

The convicts, for their part, know that their cooperation is needed for the orderly operation of the prison, and they play the guards for all they are worth. Sykes observed that if a guard attempts to enforce every regulation, he stirs up the convicts and thereby "becomes burdensome to the top officials of the prison bureaucratic staff who realize only too well that their apparent dominance rests on some degree of co-operation." The privileges accorded certain inmate leaders maintain the power equilibrium (as well as perpetuate the unofficial social structure). Therefore, Sykes concluded, the inmates themselves and not the official hierarchy handle many matters of internal control. Eventually the authorities find that much of their power has been lost to the convicts and, as Korn and McCorkle previously showed, the equilibrium is lost and friction results, with a showdown likely.

Sykes likened the Trenton riots to riots in other prisons of the period. Trenton, he said, had drifted more and more into inmate control in the 1940s. As this happened, the prison administration tried to recapture control by tightening security. Such an effort, Sykes believed, "undermines the cohesive forces at work in the inmate population and it is these forces which play a critical part in keeping the society of the prison on an even keel." The convicts who benefited from the privileges of the earlier, stable environment lose control; the more aggressive and psychopathic types assert their dominance and capitalize on the disequilibrium that the new rigidity causes. Or, as Sykes concisely stated, "The system breeds rebellion by attempting to enforce the system's rules. The custodian's efforts to secure a greater degree of control result in the destruction of that control, temporary though it may be, in those uprisings we label riots."

Neil Smelser's later theory of collective behavior and A. Smith's conflict theory of riots combined many elements of these earlier analyses.[17] Smelser posited six preconditions for a riot: 1) structural conduciveness, 2) strain or tension, 3) the growth or spread of a generalized belief, 4) a precipitation factor, 5) mobilization and organization for action, and 6) the operation of mechanisms of social control. In Smith's conflict theory, riots develop when a group or person wishes another to exercise power but the other cannot, for whatever reason. A conflict declaration follows, which must be resolved through withdrawal, bargaining, violence, or mediation.

The problem with all these functional and other analyses based on prison culture is that they accept the basic assumption that convicts who are acculturated to prison resist formal authority and become antisocial; once they are "prisonized," they supposedly lose any potential for rehabilitation. Conversely, these analyses assume that the convicts who are alienated from the inmate code and who identify with the administrative hierarchy—and obey it—are those most likely to be rehabilitated. Hence, identifying with the values of the guards becomes the same as adopting the values of free society—that is, the rule of rational laws. For the inmate to comply with formal power would therefore be healthy, and obedience becomes rehabilitation.

But obedience to power (in prison) and a sense of moral obligation to legitimate authority (in free society) are qualitatively different. Forced obedience is not the same as accepting the tenets of free society. We cannot liken prison society to free society, and we therefore cannot predict behavior outside the walls on the basis of behavior within.

The error of all these reformers is their assumption that since it was a lack of obedience to the law that got the convict in trouble in the first place, compliance in prison reflects a positive behavioral change, even if only in response to the artificial power structure of the prison. But it has been shown over and over again that some of the most hardened criminals become model prisoners. Therefore although many of these penologists made deft analyses of prison culture and advanced our knowledge of institutional life, they could not translate these studies to any real rehabilitative programs.

It is revealing to consider one major prison that did not experience a major disturbance during this period, yet that had a system totally unlike the model the criminologists advocated. Stateville Prison in Joliet, Illinois (at the time the fourth-largest prison in the nation), enjoyed stability throughout the riot years through a system of charismatic leadership, total power, and a "hierarchy of inducements."

In the late 1920s and early 1930s, Stateville had been an "open prison," one in which the inmates almost literally ran the institution because of an extraordinarily weak administration. Convicts at the time remarked that the prison tolerated gambling, drinking, protection rackets, and gangs running wild. Convict leaders literally ran the prison, while the ordinary prisoners were treated abominably. Convicts even made tar-paper sheds in the yard in which they gambled, drank, and had sex. Fights were endemic, there were knives and other weapons in most hands, and prisoners were allowed to work with any type of tools unsupervised. Guards wisely stayed away from most of this action, out of fear for their lives. They traveled through the prison only in pairs. The infamous Nathan Leopold, who was a prisoner there, called this period the "Wild West Days" of Stateville.[18]

In March 1931 the convicts rioted for no apparent reason; they went on a rampage, setting fire to the shops, smashing machinery, and inflicting violence on each other. (No one attempted an escape.) Finally the police and militia were called in to stop the spree. In 1935 a prisoner escaped simply by walking through the gates disguised as a visitor. Escapes, like riots, are the prison failures that are most newsworthy, and the media attention they capture often induces change. In this case, the governor fired the warden and hired Joseph Ragen in his stead.

Ragen ruled Stateville from 1936 to 1961. His first step was to tighten the prison. He locked everyone up for ten days and "shook down" the whole prison.[19] He confiscated several hundred weapons, including over four hundred knives more than a foot long; he fired guards, broke the "big-shot" convicts, tore down the sheds, and took other strict security measures. Ragen clamped down so absolutely and quickly that the institutional society had no chance to have the classic functional crisis. Ragen kept his system in effect so long without lightening up that the prison could not erupt into a rebellion over rising expectations. In fact, the prisoners had few expectations at all.

Ragen was no criminologist. He had had only a rudimentary education before becoming a small-town sheriff and county treasurer. He had been a politically appointed warden at Menard State Prison before taking over at Stateville. Ragen was a custodian first and last. To him, prison was a place for keeping criminals locked up and society protected. If a prisoner became "rehabilitated" in the process, so much the better, but that was not his primary concern. He put little stock in professional reformers, and they played only a small role during his reign.

Ragen literally transformed Stateville into a paramilitary institution, with himself as the supreme patriarchal authority. He installed a system of intense supervision, with numerous rules that covered every facet of prison life. The rules applied to both convicts and guards and were so comprehensive that nobody could possibly adhere to all of them. Ragen's dictum, "Stress the small things, you will never have to worry about the big ones,"[20] stood him in good stead; by focusing on enforcement of all the rules for both guards and convicts, the accommodation between authorities and prisoners and the apparently "inevitable" power struggle, as described by Gresham Sykes and others, was avoided.

Ragen created a prison universe that revolved around himself as the charismatic authority from whom all power emanates and to whom all loyalty is due. The main role of everyone in the prison, both the convicts and the guards, was to please Ragen. He believed that the only rights the convicts had were to decent food, clean clothing, and satisfactory housing. Everything else was a privilege that only Ragen had the power to bestow. This atmosphere created a hierarchy of inducements. When discipline is that strict, any little privilege is appreciated all out of proportion to its reality. And in Stateville, everything was a privilege: work assignments, having outside visitors, letter writing, even spending one's own money. Discipline was arbitrary and fierce, as the *Chicago Tribune* approvingly stated: "Discipline at Joliet-Stateville is not merely strict; like security, it is absolute. Not even the slightest infraction of the rules is tolerated. The inmates march to and from work, meals, the bath-house, the barber shop, the commissary, in a column of two's and they march in step. Profane or abusive language to employees or other inmates is not tolerated. Neither is insolence."[21] Ragen co-opted many of the tougher inmates by giving them good jobs, but they were not permitted to use the jobs to enhance their power, as at other prisons. Because discipline was so harsh, the system of small inducements kept the convicts in line. Ragen thus maintained control as a patriarch for whose favor everyone vied.

It is true that many convicts suffered emotionally and psychologically from this discipline, but they at least knew what to expect and were not subject to the almost arbitrary brutalities typical of convict power structures. As Ragen reduced his population to subservience, the world he created was a far cry from Progressive penology; neither rebellion nor rehabilitation was possible. But during his twenty-five year reign, Stateville had no riots or escapes—the two main criteria for a warden's success. When the country's prisons erupted in mass violence in the 1950s, Stateville remained calm. Joseph Ragen's success won him a place on the McGee commission to study the causes of riots.

After the riots of the 1950s, reform became fashionable in the media and among politicians. In response, Ragen simply changed his rhetoric and began referring to his system of military discipline as rehabilitation. With perverse logic, Ragen was able to redefine his system using the categories of the academic functionalists who thought obedience was the road to rehabilitation: "Ragen reasoned that the strictness of the Stateville regime would coerce the inmate into a conformity that would ultimately produce a respect for the rules. Through obedience to prison rules, the inmate would be resocialized."[22] This method was hardly what McCorkle and Korn had in mind when they denounced the "humanitarians," or what Sykes envisioned as the moral obligation to adhere to societal rules. But one cannot deny that the population of Stateville largely obeyed.

Ragen's regime at Stateville illustrates the ambiguity of the reform movement. Both the penologists and the custodians sought prisoner resocialization through acceptance of authority (in actuality, power). Although each group had a different means, what counted for both was order in prison and control of the convict population.

Ragen's prison was the exception of the period. The nation's prisons needed sweeping change and reform. The public was demanding action. The penologists and reformers set out to translate their analyses of prison conditions into concrete proposals for action. It is to these responses to prison violence that we now turn.

Chapter Four

The Decline of Treatment, 1950–1960

The spate of riots in the early 1950s brought public support for the penologists and reformers and allowed them to speed up the implementation of reforms and other experiments in the nation's prisons. The American Prison Association's report on the causes of the riots emphasized overcrowding, lack of programs, and substandard personnel, among others. In order to alleviate overcrowding and its dangers, a movement developed to build new prisons according to the classification of the individual offender by type and security risk. In addition, new programs were added, systems were overhauled, and more professionals entered the field. Penologists hailed the 1950s as the Era of Treatment, and after the riots the American Prison Association symbolically changed its name to the American Correctional Association (ACA) to underline the penal system's mission to treat or correct convicts—and not just to punish them.

Building on the analyses of the functional school, the Era of Treatment saw a greater trend toward classification of prisoners, group therapy, increased use of the indeterminate sentence, and the emergence of California as the leader in the treatment of offenders.

Although classification of convicts was introduced in the prison system in the 1930s, it did not receive general acceptance until the late 1940s and saw widespread implementation only in the 1950s. *Classification* meant two things to treatment-oriented penologists: 1) segregation of convicts according to different levels of security (i.e., minimum, medium, and maximum), and 2) diagnosis of convicts according to type of criminality and individual treatment using behavior-modification programs.

Classification for security stemmed from the functional analysts' concept of prisonization. Segregation of prisoners according to security risk would isolate the most "prisonized" convicts and rupture the prison community's unofficial social structure, with its harmful effects on the majority of convicts. Placing lesser offenders in medium and minimum security facilities would allow the treatment staff to orient them more effectively to outside, free-society values.

The ACA even approved maximum numbers of prisoners per state for the three different security levels. No more than 35 percent of a state's prisoners should reside in a maximum security institution, the association declared; perhaps only 2 percent of all convicts are so dangerous and incorrigible that they need supersecurity provisions. The ACA thought that no more than twelve hundred prisoners should reside in an adult prison, even a maximum security one. Medium security institutions should contain at least 25 percent of convicts, and minimum security prisons or work camps (called rehabilitation camps in many states) should have no less than 20 percent. (By the end of the 1950s, however, statistics show fifty-three prisons with over twelve hundred prisoners, and almost all of these were maximum security institutions.[1])

Although the reality was far different from the ideal, most states accepted the concept of classification by the end of the 1950s, and many spent the decade attempting—if not succeeding—in implementing various methods of classifying prisoners.

The ACA's 1947 *Handbook on Classification* spelled out the objectives of classification:

The purposes of classification are accomplished first, by analyzing the problems presented by the individual through the use of every available technique, such as thorough social investigation, medical, psychiatric, psychological examinations, educational and vocational, religious and recreational studies; second, by deciding in staff conference upon a program of treatment and training based upon these analyses; third, by assuring that the program decided upon is placed into operation; and fourth, by observing the progress of the inmate under this program and by changing it when indicated.[2]

These goals were ambitious, and few prisons could successfully achieve them. One drawback of the ideal classification program was that in order to classify properly, states needed not only professional personnel but graded prisons. Building new prisons to segregate the various classes of prisoners was the most expensive aspect of the classification process. The public wanted to lock up felons but did not want to spend approximately $11,000 per convict in construction costs to build them. (The sum today, of course, is much higher; so is the cost of yearly maintenance of prisoners.) At the end of the decade, pre-1900 prisons were still standing in forty-one jurisdictions, and between 1940 and 1960 only eighteen states built new "correctional centers." Most of the new prisons were built on the Sing Sing and Auburn systems, in the old maximum-security-fortress style. Thus, the security-classification process was doomed to failure, if only for lack of physical plant.

Nevertheless, several states did recognize the need to segregate convicts according to crimes, personalities, and security risk. While most of these jurisdictions reorganized their prisons with the aim of segregating security types within the same walls, some attempted more ambitious projects or built new institutions.

In New England, with a smaller population than other regions and therefore a smaller number of prisoners, the states concentrated their efforts on regionalizing classification. For instance, Rhode Island received transfers of adult male felons from neighboring states, while adult females went to institutions in Massachusetts. In other states it was not so simple. New prisons had to be built in some; most states that did not put up new buildings had to supply separate areas either within existing prisons or in locations outside for the initial classification process.

This procedure was one of the more important features of the new penology. Before an inmate could be sent to a certain type of prison and receive an individualized treatment program, he had to go through what were called reception and diagnostic centers. These names themselves were obvious manifestations of the medical model of treatment. Staff within institutions could receive and diagnose, and after a period of quarantine the convict was placed in an institution's program. The classification for security could also be carried out in an independent diagnostic institution that places prisoners in graded prisons for programs and treatment. Many states had to create such centers anew; Colorado opened one in 1957, and Alabama, Illinois, Massachusetts, Kentucky, Washington, Rhode Island, Michigan, Pennsylvania, Minnesota, and New Jersey did so by the end of the 1950s. Others, such as Kansas in 1961, did so in the early 1960s. The Federal Bureau of Prisons set up its own facilities during the same period. Some of these reception centers were used strictly for juvenile offenders, some for adults, and a few for both. In some southern and western states, such as Texas and New Mexico, the reception and diagnostic process lacked any sophistication whatever, and prisoners were classified simply by race.

In medical terms, the staff diagnosed the "illness" of the convict and then prescribed a "cure." The objectives of reception were

1. the study of the personality and social background of the newly committed inmates by a competent professional staff;

2. the screening of prisoners for assignment to particular institutions and to special segregation units in terms of their needs and the custodial provisions of the institutions;

3. the planning of a program of individual treatment for consideration by the staff of the receiving institution;

4. the preparation of individual case studies of value in the assignment to work in the maintenance of the prison and in correctional industries in accordance with individual needs and institutional provisions;

5. recognition of the prison subversives and the psychopaths, and recommendation of individualized programs to prevent escapes, assaultive behavior, arson, and other destruction of property, and other incidents unfortunate both for the inmate and the institution.[3]

Several problems arose that were associated with the classification process. A common problem was that classifiers did not take into consideration the facilities and competencies of the future host institutions. For instance, a diagnostic center could prescribe a comprehensive treatment program and then send the convict to a prison that was totally inadequate to handle the prescription. Probably the most important problem was that concern for custody took precedence over providing a treatment program. If a convict was considered a security risk, he went to a maximum security institution no matter what treatment was prescribed.

The American Correctional Association promulgated standards for classification in its 1947 *Handbook of Classification* and later revised them in the 1959 edition, *A Manual of Correctional Standards*. It recommended at least sixty days for a proper diagnosis of prisoners; a minimum staff of seventy-five to handle a weekly intake of twenty-five to thirty convicts; and enough interviews and tests not only to determine the proper treatment program but also to acclimate the convict to prison life *and* lay an affirmative attitude for what awaited him. Failure was built into this system, for even if a diagnostic center's staff actually made a convincing case for treating a newly inducted prisoner, the reality of doing time was frequently much different from therapy.

Another problem affecting the diagnostic center was staffing. The professional and custodial staffing levels advocated by the ACA were actually reached only in rare instances. In 1960, Chester L. Chiles of Washington State surveyed diagnostic center procedures and found that only one reported having adequate staff to handle its duties. Fourteen of thirty-six institutions relied on their own personnel for classification rather than on professionals in a reception center. Only two institutions reported that they could provide recommended treatments. (This survey depended on voluntary information, however, and the data are not necessarily accurate.) In 1954, Harry Elmer Barnes and Negley Teeters reported that there were a total of 385 full- and part-time professionals working in correctional treatment. In 1958, Alfred Schnur stated that out of 26,938 people employed full time in state and federal prisons and reformatories, only 1,337 dealt with treatment. Schnur broke this figure down in the following way: to treat 161,587 prisoners, there were twenty-three psychiatrists, ninety-six institutional parole officers, 257 case workers, and 739 academic, vocational, and trade teachers.[4] Considering the number of prisoners in institutions, the amount of time each could receive in treatment was minuscule. In other words, actual treatments did not even approximate the ACA standards.

Not only did these institutions lack staff, it is questionable whether the methods they used in diagnosis had validity. The diagnostic tools were based primarily on behavioral, psychiatric, and social science principles and were not nearly as reliable as the medical diagnoses they emulated. In fact, during the 1950s many of the staff at these centers were steeped in psychiatric methods, and their aim was to make the incoming convicts aware of their deep-seated psychiatric problems. Even if such methods worked for convicts, the ratio of professionals to convicts was so small that intensive psychoanalysis had little chance of success.

In contrast to the high-minded prose of the treatment-oriented penologists of the period, it is enlightening to hear the viewpoint of a prisoner on his experiences in one reception and diagnostic center. Malcolm Braly spent more than twenty years in a variety of prisons, especially in California, and wrote one of the more insightful convict memoirs of the period. He escaped from the Carson City, Nevada, prison and was captured after a shoot-out in California. He was sent to San Quentin, where he spent three months being classified in what was called a guidance center.

He underwent batteries of tests, orientation classes, and the like. As he writes,

We quickly learned we were expected to view this journey as a quest, and the object of our quest was to discover our problem. It was assumed we were here because of psychological problems, and our task now, by which we could expect to be judged, was to isolate and come to terms with them. Boys who had stolen cars were thought to be acting out a symbolic return to the womb and once they had been helped to understand their true motivation and recognize its utter futility they would be free of the compulsion. I mock this now, even if I didn't mock it then, but it's not the most basic notion at which I will invite you to laugh with me, but simply at the grotesque extensions which sometimes flourished here in the California Department of Corrections. And no matter what your private opinion, when the Adult Authority, the remote body authorized to grant parole, asked in tones of high seriousness if you had come to grips with your problem, you were willing to concede you might have a problem even if you had to invent one on the spot.[5]

Such realism from a then-young convict quickly deflates the theories of penologists who were seriously attempting to break down the defenses of their charges. Braly's theme is not new, however. When Alexis de Tocqueville and Gustave de Beaumont visited American penitentiaries in 1831, they noted, "The criminal, therefore, has an interest in showing to the chaplain, with whom alone he has moral communications, profound repentance for his crime, and a lively desire to return to virtue. If these sentiments are not sincere, he nevertheless will profess them."[6]

As for instilling positive attitudes in prisoners about their forthcoming prison experience, Braly remarks, "The orientation classes were interesting and useful for a while. We heard volumes as to how prisons *did* function from the cons. Penny [the guidance counselor] told us how it was *supposed* to function, and we were in a position to adjust the disparity."[7]

Perhaps the most damning statement Braly makes reveals his attitude toward the entire prison experience: "We knew the Care-and-Treatment types and Custody were all buddies together out there at the officers' snack bar."[8] For the truth of the matter was—and still is—that the primary objective of incarceration is to lock up the convict, despite the rhetoric of rehabilitation. Custodial matters came first in the earliest prisons and still came first through every change in prison orientation. No matter what programs the professionals used to "treat" convicts, everybody knew that in the last analysis custody always took precedence, in the view of both the correctional system and the public. The concept of rehabilitation is fine, but it takes a back seat to public safety; and public safety means order and no riots or escapes.

Other prison memoirists share Braly's attitude toward the treatment received in prison. Nevertheless, the 1950s saw the heyday of experimentation in many of the techniques the Progressives had only dreamed about. Treatment became fashionable. In addition to reception and diagnostic centers and security-segregated "correctional centers," totally different types of institutions emerged. The two best known were Patuxent in Maryland and Highfields in New Jersey.

Patuxent was perhaps the most extreme manifestation of the medical model of correction. Opened in 1955 under Maryland's defective delinquent statute for extremely violent and mentally troubled offenders, it was operated entirely by psychiatrists, who created what they called a "therapeutic milieu." The psychiatrists experimented with a variety of techniques, primarily group therapy. Patuxent relied exclusively on the indeterminate sentence; this meant that once a team of psychiatrists had declared a convict "cured," he was released from prison. Using their techniques, it was very difficult to prove "health" in the same sense as a broken arm is healed. Even though many supposedly foolproof tests were used, a prison-smart convict could usually manipulate the treatment staff to his advantage. (Braly describes "beating" the Minnesota Multiphasic Personality Test in San Quentin.) Many prisoners who were serving determinate life sentences in Maryland maximum security institutions schemed incessantly to get into Patuxent so they could get cured.

Patuxent was organized on the "graded-tier" system, with four levels. Like prisoners in Alexander Maconochie's nineteenth-century graded system, Patuxent prisoners started out at the bottom with virtually no privileges and in solitary confinement. They were promoted and given additional privileges when the staff believed they had manifested socially acceptable behavior. The fourth or top level gave them extensive privileges and benefits. The staff could also demote a prisoner at will. The climax, of course, was the day when the convict was declared cured and no longer a defective delinquent.

The other side of the coin of an institution like Patuxent was that it was possible for a prisoner never to be declared cured and to spend the rest of his life there. A convict with an indeterminate life sentence could spend considerably more time in Patuxent than in an institution where he would usually receive a parole after, say, ten years. For almost half the prisoners, that is exactly what happened. Between 1955 and 1965,

46 percent of the 135 convicts paroled had served more time than they would have in traditional institutions. Even more telling, only about 12 percent were actually declared "cured."[9] Three times as many left through the recommitment hearings that they were granted after realizing Patuxent offered little hope of early release. In 1971, Patuxent's therapeutic milieu was restricted by the courts, and the staff was forced to write disciplinary codes and restrict "negative reinforcement" techniques—a euphemism for solitary confinement. For the desperate long-termer, however, it still seemed worthwhile to try the Patuxent cure.

The other well-known treatment institution of the 1950s was the juvenile delinquent home in Highfields, New Jersey. The Highfields "experiment," as it was called, was intended to create for youthful offenders an atmosphere of rehabilitation using group interaction based on psychological and sociological conceptions. As the director stated, "The whole Highfields experience is directed toward piercing through these strong defenses against rehabilitation, toward undermining delinquent attitudes, and toward developing a self-conception favorable to reformation. The sessions on guided group interaction are especially directed to achieve this objective."[10] This approach resembled the group methods used by self-help organizations such as Alcoholics Anonymous, who believe that those who help themselves are capable of helping others. The originators of the experiment compared recidivist rates at Highfields with those of Annandale, another reformatory in New Jersey, and considered Highfields the more successful. Other studies using more variables contested these rates but found that Highfields was at least cheaper to run—and in the context of U.S. prison politics, that is success indeed.[11]

Highfields is also notable as an illustration of another prison reform trend of the 1950s—the use of professional penologists as directors of penal institutions. Donald Clemmer in Washington, D.C., was one; sociologist Lloyd McCorkle ran Highfields, then went on to become the warden at Clinton Prison in New Jersey. Clarence Schrag directed several institutions in Washington state. Other sociologists and criminologists took such positions, especially in California. Once the professionals had their chance to change the system, they had difficulty excusing its failure in the future.

Patuxent and Highfields were but extreme examples of methods used in penitentiaries and reformatories throughout the nation. Psychiatric group therapy techniques infiltrated most state institutions in the 1950s. At the beginning of the decade, a survey showed that 109 out of 312 institutions were experimenting with some kind of group treatment; by the end of the decade all had at least tried it. This meant that once an offender had passed through a reception center (where he was introduced to group treatment) and was classified and placed in an institution, his in-house treatment consisted of regular group meetings. In most cases attendance was mandatory, since once officials embrace and accept a prison routine, it tends to become part of the prison's regime and hence is rarely voluntary.

The objective of all this was, once again, to acclimate prisoners to the mores and restrictions of free society. In the process defined by the theory of the prison as a social community, the prisoner gains values from his peer group. Once released, the ex-convict can be assimilated into free society and become a useful citizen: "the major objective of correctional treatment should be the internalization and self-enforcement of social values by the individual. This process cannot be enforced by an external authority to which the inmate is hostile, and that the person will only internalize the values of a group with which he can identify."[12]

This process, called "guided group interaction" in New Jersey, involves "the use of free discussion to reeducate the delinquent to accept the restrictions of society and to find satisfaction in conforming to social norms."[13] Ideally, the group therapy session is led by a professional psychiatrist or psychologist. He structures a social experience in which he and the convicts freely discuss and analyze problems. These discussions give the convict insight into his lack of adjustment to societal norms. The group climate is mutually supportive and allows the convicts freedom to find their roles in the group. The outcome is problem resolution and access to the road to social conformity. The group should be small, should meet regularly for forty-five minutes to two hours a session and from two to five times a week, should be homogeneous in terms of age, education, and intelligence, should encourage voluntary participation, and should have little turnover. If all of these conditions are met, then the goal "of strengthening the inmate by enabling him to find means of helping himself is reinforced and made meaningful by its integration into the total program of the institution."[14]

Little of this happened in practice. Few, if any, prisons had the well-trained group leaders called for. The poorly trained counselors who did lead the sessions probably did more harm than good. One of the most crucial tenets of classical psychotherapy, voluntarism, rarely existed in the prison setting; most prisoners participated only because they rightly assumed that if they did not, it would be held against them: it would show that the prisoner had not recognized his antisocial values, was totally prisonized, and was unwilling to change or conform. On the other hand, he was led to believe that participation could lead to an early parole.

Moreover, participation and discussion in most sessions was not free and open because the convict knew that much of what he said was being recorded by the leader. Therefore, the prisoner was constantly on his guard against saying anything meaningful that might harm his chances for release. The consequence was that little of value came out of these sessions, and most were a waste of time. Malcolm Braly, in his novel *On the Yard*, describes one such session:

He found his group already gathered, sitting in the usual symbolic circle. The therapist, a Dr. Erlenmeyer, occupied what was intended as just one more chair, but the group automatically polarized wherever he seated himself. He was dressed entirely in shades of brown, and his shirt was darker than his coat. His glasses were tinted a pale tan, and his head full of hair seemed soft and dusty.

"You're late, Paul," he said, in a tone that didn't admit the obvious quality of his remark. His voice was opaque.

"I lost track of the day," Juleson said.

This hung in the air for a moment like a palpable lie, then settled into the heavy silence. The group had nothing going. No one, as they said, was coming out with anything. Juleson settled around in his chair, careful not to look at Erlenmeyer, who might try to make him feel responsible for this wasteful silence. Once Erlenmeyer had stressed how therapy was working on them even while they sat dumb, as sometimes happened, for the hour. But he didn't like their silences. . . .

Finally, Erlenmeyer cleared his throat to ask, "Why do you suppose Paul is late so often?"

They looked at each other to see if anyone were going to attempt an answer. Bernard only shrugged; he didn't care. After a moment, Zekekowski said quietly, "He's got better sense than the rest of us."[15]

Not all group therapy sessions worked like Braly's fictional one. But lacking staff, few could actually work out problems in a meaningful way. And if some prisoners received individual psychiatric therapy, their number relative to the whole was minute.

Educational and vocational programs of the 1950s fared somewhat better, if only from an institutional point of view. Most institutions started elementary and high school programs, and a few even had college courses. A variety of trades were taught, including cooking, baking, butchering, auto mechanics, printing, welding, and so on. Few prisoners learned the trades, however, and many were employed in state-use industries for governmental purposes, which gave them few job prospects outside the walls. A California survey noted that only 36 percent of parolees had received any trade training in prison, and only 12 percent of those worked in a field related to that training on the outside.[16] Since California's penology was relatively progressive, other states most likely had lower rates.

Vocational programs did, however, aid the custodial and budgetary state of the prison system. State-use industries grew in the 1950s; the value of state-use production increased by 50 percent, from $52 million to $101 million.[17] Actual convict employment figures were not so impressive, increasing by only a small percentage; but prisons actively created industries and programs, if only to keep prisoners busy. Since pervasive idleness is one of the most dangerous features of prison life, increased employment opportunities and programs enabled the custodial staff to keep the prison population under better control and to obviate tensions that might otherwise lead to riots.

The main reason that most of these treatment programs were extended was the widespread use of the indeterminate sentence in the 1950s. The Progressive ideal of professional criminologists, psychiatrists, and the like rather than the judges determining sentences of prisoners came true in many jurisdictions, and the prisoner's participation in these programs was the primary way to evaluate his progress toward "normality."

California made the most extensive use of the indeterminate sentence (except for specialized institutions such as Patuxent), and that state came to the forefront of penology in the 1950s. In 1944, Governor Earl Warren brought in Richard McGee, former warden at Riker's Island (New York) and commissioner of corrections for the state of Washington, as California's head of corrections. At the same time, Warren overhauled the state's penal system by authorizing the construction of diversified prisons and by creating the Adult Authority to classify, distribute, treat, and determine releases for California's prisoners. McGee brought in Norman Fenton, a Stanford sociologist, to run the classification and treatment programs, and he in turn recruited other academics to aid him in formulating new procedures.

California became the nation's leading light in penology under McGee's tenure. As the noted psychiatrist Karl Menninger wrote,

The California correctional system . . . has been far out in the lead among the states, with excellent programs of work, education, vocational training, medical services, group counseling, and other rehabilitative activities. A notable feature is the combination of diagnosis, evaluation, treatment, and classification. . . . This constitutes a systematic effort along scientific principles to ascertain from collected case history data and from firsthand examination just what the assets and liabilities of the floundering individual are.[18]

During this era, even convicts initially had a certain amount of enthusiasm for the new treatment programs. John Irwin, who did time in San Quentin and later became a sociologist, remarks in his book *The Felon* that convicts

were led to believe that they would be able to raise their educational level to at least the fifth grade and much higher if they desired, to learn a trade, to have physical defects, disfigurations, and tattoos removed or corrected, and to receive help in various individual and group therapy programs in solving their psychological problems. In effect they were led to believe that if they participated in prison programs with sincerity and resolve they would leave prison in better condition than they entered and would generally be much better equipped to cope with the outside world.[19]

Once the convicts had entered many of these treatment programs, however, it did not take them long to become disillusioned. They thought the staff hypocritical, distrusted their motives, and reacted to being labeled "sick" and in need of cure under the medical model. Perhaps most important, they resented the arbitrariness and authoritarianism of the Adult Authority.

The Adult Authority was composed of nine members who were appointed to four-year terms by the governor. By 1950, the Adult Authority wielded almost complete power over sentencing and releasing prisoners. It was believed at that time that such power was necessary to implement rehabilitation programs and to determine whether a convict had completed the proper course of treatment and was ready to reenter free society. The Adult Authority had the power to set all sentences, within the statutory limits for particular crimes. Such limits could be one to ten years for grand larceny, five to life for first-degree robbery, or ten to life for murder. Within these broad limits, the authority had complete discretion to set the sentence and to parole. The panel of experts in turn relied on an institution's professional staff's reports on their charges to make these determinations. The law made no requirement for due process or review of decisions. California thus performed the experiment that the

Progressives had called for: professionals decided when rehabilitation had taken place.

In reality, the system worked arbitrarily, and the prisoner rarely knew exactly when he would be released until his sentence had been served. He appeared annually for review before the board; the board did not have to set a term, and the convict was usually kept in perpetual suspense on how much time he would serve. No written guidelines or procedures were kept, and if a person was turned down for parole, no reason was given. How did he eventually find out when he would be released? The Authority told him.

Much of what went on in Adult Authority hearings was a repetition of what went on in parole hearings during the Progressive period. Although the board was supposed to read staff reports concerning progress toward rehabilitation, in reality, as we have seen, the professionals had little idea whether a person had had a positive character change or not. Furthermore, each prisoner had only a ten- to thirty-minute interview before the board—not enough time to adequately assess any part of the convict's behavior, much less his "rehabilitation": "Only one board member really deals with any one convict. Each board member takes a few minutes to read the inmate's file, during the time when a previous inmate is being questioned. As each inmate walks in, the board member usually asks a few perfunctory questions and the inmate is dismissed. Over 80 per cent of the inmates are turned down the first time they appear for parole, and the percentage drops only slightly with each later attempt."[20]

The authority relied extensively on a file on the convict that the professional staff kept throughout his prison career. The file was filled with reports on the prisoner's behavior and development in prison. But the staff was required only to present descriptive and evaluative reports and was not allowed to recommend a disposition. Once again, little indication could exist of how the convict would behave in free society if released.

For his part, the convict knew that his actions in prison would determine his release, and he acted accordingly. Any disciplinary problems would work against him. As in the parole hearings of the 1930s, past crimes could be taken into consideration, besides the crime for which he had been convicted. If he pleaded innocent, it indicated a lack of remorse and no character reform. His looks, age, and other superficial factors were important. The indeterminate sentence turned out to be one more mechanism for keeping control in prison.

Any untoward behavior could lengthen the time he served, while being a model prisoner on the surface could hasten parole. The board and the convicts knew this, and they both played the game. For the prisoner, however, it was one of the worst facets of prison life, because he never really knew when he would get out. Moreover, under indeterminate sentencing, the median term served by a convict in California went up, not down. California prisoners have reported that the worst feature of prison life was not the poor conditions—food, medical care, idleness—but the arbitrariness of the parole bureaucracy—the Adult Authority.

When Malcom Braly appeared for the first time before the Adult Authority during his first stint in San Quentin, he was a young first-termer. "I appeared in front of the Adult Authority after I pulled a year. It was the only time I came before these men with anything like an advantage. I had already served a lot of time, longer, it could be argued, than I should have considering my intent, which, of course, was impossible to verify, but I was young, and very blue-eyed and White American, and, in appearance, at least, I might have been a wayward son from one of their own homes. The members regarded me with some sympathy."[21] A few years later, Braly appeared again before the board, but this time he had been classified a third-termer and was serving at Folsom, a maximum security prison for hard-core felons.

We never knew just how long we would have to serve—my own basic sentence was one year to life, which left the A.A. a lot of time to play with—but most of us knew in a general way about how much time we would do. There was nothing that interested us more and we logged years trying to thrash out a basis on which to predict the Adult Authority. This was our great debate. We knew which programs to try to associate ourselves with and we knew which ploys were now exhausted. We could gauge public pressure and the changing winds of penal philosophy, and we knew which individual members were apt to be liberal and which were conservative. We charted their idiosyncracies. We hoped they were feeling well.[22]

It is obvious that the rhetoric of the Karl Menningers did not reflect the realities of serving under California's Adult Authority. When treatment policies came under severe attack during the 1960s (see chapter 5), the Adult Authority in particular was singled out for damnation. A report on its policies stated,

The time that an individual spends in prison seems to depend on three factors: (1) The values and feelings of individual parole board members. (2) The "mood" of the public. (3) Institution population pressures. . . . The parole board operates without a clear and rationally justified policy. Responsibility for decisions involving deep considerations of justice, public safety, and cost is vested in a board legally and scientifically unequipped to justify *any* policy toward less serious offenders. As a result, California general parole policy, reflecting emotion, not facts, has become increasingly conservative, punitive, and expensive.[23]

Nonetheless, other jurisdictions rushed to emulate the California experiment. Minnesota and Michigan attempted to implement some of California's programs. James Bennett, director of the Federal Bureau of Prisons, pushed for the adoption of the Indeterminate Sentence Act of 1958 to make classification procedures more meaningful. Under the act, parole was allowed after the completion of one-third of the sentence, provided that the staff recommended it. Almost all the states were at least paying lip service to group therapy. In California, under McGee and Fenton in 1956, five thousand prisoners were enrolled in such sessions. The program was extended throughout the system, and attendance at meetings was mandatory for a time.

In spite of all these programs and attempts at rehabilitation, recidivism rates remained high, and the prisons still were not working. Could this mean that "treatment" on the medical model was invalid? In a spate of articles the professionals argued that it was valid: the programs would be successful if they got enough political and professional support. Since some statistics showed that small, intensive efforts manifested glimmerings of hope, large-scale programs would succeed if they were only given a chance. Alfred Schnur in a 1958 article blamed the failure of the New Penology on lack of such support: "What kinds of professional people, and how many, have been hired to implement the new penology and achieve its goals?" he asked rhetorically. "Not many!"[24] He answered the question of whether it worked, "I don't know. It has not been tried!" In 1959, Lloyd McCorkle and Richard Korn perceptively noted that although the advocates of rehabilitation had succeeded on an ideological and educational level, they had created problems by raising expectations to unreasonable levels. The public had started to believe that prisoners could be rehabilitated but was disillusioned when crime continued at ever growing rates. Korn and McCorkle called for more professional support and concluded on an unrealistic note by saying, "The Era of Treatment remains stalled at the threshold, an age still clamoring to be born."[25]

The truth of the matter was that the Era of Treatment, far from "about to be born," was in its death throes. The Progressive penologists had predicated rehabilitation on having convicts accept the tenets of free, normal society; attaining this goal depended upon using various behavioral or psychiatric methods to break down criminal values and replacing them with values associated with free society. The insoluble problem was to instill free-society normality in a caged population. Ironically, when free-society values really began to infiltrate the prison community, it meant the end of the treatment era. In the 1960s, free society experienced the civil rights movement, antiwar activity, the radicalization of college students and youth in general, and a general shift to the left in politics. The idea of demanding "rights" entered prisons, as did many radical prisoners. Racial and political strife ensued, and in the process treatment was seen for the control method it actually was. Penology, like many prisoners, became radicalized. It is to this period of ferment that we now turn.

FORLORN HOPE.

What wish can bless, or supplicating pray'r
Prosper the wretch who joys t' inflict despair?
These bars—these bolts—where mis'ry lies confin'd,
Can furnish food to feast the poison'd mind.
Here each endures, while yet he draws his breath,
A stroke more fatal than the scythe of death.

JAIL.

Postcard, "Convicts at Dinner, the Ohio Penitentiary." *Collection of the author*

Prisoners learning the trade of knitting, Sing Sing Prison, New York, 1915. *Library of Congress*

Delaware State Penitentiary whipping post and stocks, ca. 1907. Delaware was the last state in America to retain whipping as a punishment in prison. Although the last whipping took place on 16 June 1952, the law was not repealed until 6 July 1972. Maryland only legally abolished whipping for wife beaters in 1952. *Library of Congress*

An example of the convict leasing system, Pitt County, North Carolina. *Library of Congress*

Eastern Penitentiary, Philadelphia, John Haviland, architect. Lithograph by J.T. Bowen (1840); J.C. Wild, artist. From *Views of Philadelphia and its Vicinity* Philadelphia: J.T. Bowen, 1848. *Collection of the author*

A satirical view of the parole system: "Now be a real good boy," Herbert Johnson, artist; between 1912 and 1941. *Library of Congress*

Federal Parole Board hearing. *National Archives*

Postcard, "Going to Yard," Iowa State Penitentiary. *Collection of the author*

Postcard, Illinois State Prison at
Joliet. *Collection of the author*

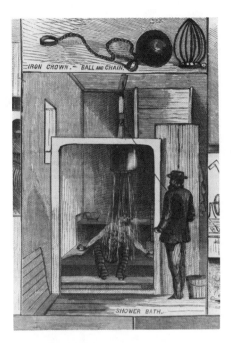

The shower bath, iron crown, and ball and chain. From "Life of a Convict at Sing Sing Prison," *Harper's Weekly,* 22 June 1867. *Collection of the author.*

Postcard, prison cells, Mansfield, Ohio, Reformatory. *Collection of the author*

Women's Prison, Sing Sing. From "Life of a Convict at Sing Sing Prison," *Harper's Weekly,* 22 June 1867. *Collection of the author*

A forlorn view from a cell. *National Archives*

Chapter Five

Corrections in Transition, 1960–1970

In the middle of the 1950s, the ideology, if not the reality, of rehabilitation was firmly rooted in the practices of therapeutic treatment, either psychotherapy or group interaction methodology. By the end of the 1960s, however, political, social, and racial events had called into question the whole idea of rehabilitation.

The treatment model of corrections had moved away from the pure utilitarianism of the early penitentiary to a brand of environmental determinism. The offender would be treated and society would be protected by locking up the worst criminals until they were deemed "cured." This Progressive model culminated in the widespread adoption of the indeterminate sentence, best exemplified by the California Adult Authority. The indeterminate sentence allowed professional criminologists and penologists to try to rehabilitate character, however long it took. By 1960, states such as California had gone a long way in taking the criminal justice process out of the hands of judges and putting it into the hands of behavioral "experts" who had the final authority to proclaim the cure and therefore the release of the offender.

Zebulon Brockway, the first superintendent of Elmira Reformatory, one of the original treatment institutions, would have been proud of this development. As far back as 1912, he had commented,

The common notion of moral responsibility based on freedom should no longer be made a foundation principle for criminal laws, court procedure, and prison treatment. The claim of such responsibility need neither be denied nor affirmed, but put aside as being out of place in a system of treatment of offenders for the purpose of public protection. Together with abrogation of this responsibility goes, too, any awesome regard for individual liberty of choice and action by imprisoned criminals. Their habitual conduct and indeed their related character must needs be directed and really determined by their legalized custodians. . . . The perfected reformatory will be the receptacle and refinery of antisocial humans who are held in custody under discretional indeterminateness for the purpose of public protection. . . . The change will be, in short, a change from the reign of sentiment swerved by the feelings to a passionless scientific procedure pursuing welfare.[1]

Although the system did not go to the extreme of total indeterminacy, almost all jurisdictions accepted the concept of individualized treatment. Parole, one of the bedrocks of the system, was practiced in every state by the 1960s. (In contrast, the Wickersham report of 1931 had reported that twenty states had no parole boards.) As we have seen, however, the realities of the parole board differed widely from jurisdiction to jurisdiction.

In spite of vast discrepancies in treatment practice, most penologists pressed for more staff and programs to rehabilitate the offender. The general slogan became "Let the punishment fit the criminal, not the crime." Acceptance of this slogan gave wide discretionary powers to those in control of penal institutions; the most extreme example was the use of the absolute indeterminate sentence at Patuxent in Maryland (see chapter 4).

In the 1960s, penologists continued this quest for scientific methods of treating offenders. Most states now had diagnostic and classification centers, and their existence was an accepted fact of the correctional process. A thorough diagnosis of an incoming convict depended on well-developed classification programs that collected data on the prisoner, predicted his or her behavior in prison, and assigned appropriate treatment programs and custodial categories.

Although many different theories of rehabilitation were abroad at the beginning of the 1960s, the most popular ones were variations of prominent criminologist Edwin Sutherland's theory of "differential association." Sutherland had developed the theory in the third edition of his text *Principles of Criminology* in 1939; he modified it in 1947, and it became a mainstay in subsequent editions. Revised and updated by prominent criminologist Donald Cressey, the book was still used as a basic text in criminology courses through the 1970s. In the 1940s a few of Sutherland's followers attempted to develop programs based on his theory, and in the late 1950s and especially in the 1960s, more and more penologists and criminologists devised typologies of convicts and treatment programs using variations of "differential association." In the 1960s it became one of the most accepted theories of criminality, and a plethora of criminologists, penologists, and sociologists were defending, attacking, testing, and conducting replication studies.

The text's seventh edition of 1966, coauthored by Cressey (Sutherland died in 1950), outlines the main points of differential association:

1. Criminal behavior is learned.
2. Criminal behavior is learned in interaction with other persons in a process of communication.
3. The principal part of the learning of criminal behavior occurs within intimate personal groups.
4. When criminal behavior is learned, the learning includes
   (a) techniques of committing the crime, which are sometimes very complicated, sometimes very simple;
   (b) the specific direction of motives, drives, rationalizations, and attitudes.
5. The specific direction of motives and drives is learned from definitions of the legal codes as favorable or unfavorable.
6. A person becomes delinquent because of an excess of definitions favorable to violation of law over definitions unfavorable to violation of law.
7. Differential associations may vary in frequency, duration, priority, and intensity.
8. The process of learning criminal behavior by association with criminal and anti-criminal patterns involves all of the mechanisms that are involved in any other learning.[2]

Sutherland further posited a principle of normative conflict, which stated that "high crime rates occurred in societies and groups characterized by conditions that lead to the development of extensive criminal subcultures." Normative conflict, according to Sutherland, explains the differences among societies' crime rates. In short, differential group organization translates into normative conflict, which accounts for crime rates, while differential association determines the individual's criminal behavior.

In 1960 Richard A. Cloward and Lloyd E. Ohlin, in their book *Delinquency and Opportunity,* put forth their idea of "differential opportunity."[3] Differential opportunity was a variation on Sutherland's theory that also drew on Robert Merton's assertion that crime can be induced by culturally instilling social objectives conducive to criminal behavior; individuals adapt to the cultural milieu that leads to crime.[4] Cloward and Ohlin took Merton's idea and formulated a typology of lower-class youths that was to be predictive of delinquency. Based on the authors' belief that everyone wants to enter their definition of the middle class, the most delinquent youth is the one who wants middle-class wealth without enduring delayed gratification, hard work, or other traditional means to gain it. Therefore, he steals.

Delinquency and Opportunity was a most influential book in the 1960s, and the authors were brought into the federal government to help revise delinquency policy. Their efforts helped bring about the Juvenile Delinquency and Control Act of 1961, which emphasized improvements in education, job opportunities, and community milieus.

Another variation of Sutherland's theory was Robert Burgess and Ronald Akers's "differential association–reinforcement theory of criminal behavior."[5] Building on B. F. Skinner's behaviorism as well, the authors argued that both social and antisocial behavior is learned and that "deviant behavior can be expected to the extent that it has been differentially reinforced over alternative behavior . . . and is defined as desirable or justified."

Another explanation of crime that began to reach prominence in the 1960s and gained increasing acceptance among sociologists was labeling theory. Foreshadowed by Frederic Thrasher in his 1927 book *The Gang* and called the "dramatization of evil" by Frank Tannenbaum in his 1938 book *Crime and Community,* labeling theory was fully developed by Edward Lemert in his 1951 book *Social Pathology.* According to labeling theory, society stigmatizes deviants, who are "a product of differentiating and isolating processes."[6] Lemert's theory recognized primary and secondary deviancy. Primary deviants are those whom racism, poverty, and the like force into crime. The primary deviant never really chooses deviancy, but society labels him a deviant because of prevailing social conditions or beliefs. The primary deviant who then accepts that image and commits himself to act according to society's label becomes a secondary deviant. Similarly, Albert Cohen, in his 1955 book *Delinquent Boys,* asserted that lower-class children, rejected by middle-class society, enter deviant subcultures because of the bourgeoisie's perception of them, and they accept values inimical to the dominant class.[7]

In sum, most of these theories define criminals and criminality in terms of existing social relationships, social interaction patterns, cultural alternatives, or ideologies. Criminals eventually define themselves in terms of an interpretive framework originally *other* than their own because of their negative socialization experiences. And this self-definition favors violation of the law.

All these sociologists based their theories on the assumption that everybody wants to enter the great American middle class. It did not cross their minds that non-middle-class people might choose a crime-free proletarian culture instead of a criminal environment if given the choice. The criminologists of this generation would not or could not understand the new world forced upon them, even as free society and hence prisoners became more radicalized as the 1960s progressed. Throughout most of the 1960s their methods held sway over prison treatment.

It is not difficult to see how differential association and labeling theory affected the study and treatment of prisoners. There was a logical progression from the environmentalism of the Progressives, with their concern for the community life of criminals and convicts, to differential association and labeling theory. Both emphasize community and social contexts. Common to both, for example, is the "stigmatized" ex-convict who cannot get a job or otherwise function in free society by the very fact that he is an ex-convict and therefore returns to crime.

In prisoner treatment, the emphasis therefore remained on therapy in a community environment. There was a greater reliance on classification data, typologies of offenders, and treatment differentials corresponding to social and cultural differences among offenders. Penologists developed differential treatment programs based on the etiology of crime and the heterogeneity of offenders. Treatment was firmly based on differentials and community-context programs. The idea of the therapeutic milieu remained the operative treatment philosophy until the 1970s.

Extending and expanding on the group therapy methods developed in the 1950s, more and more penologists advocated milieu management and environmental change programs: "Milieu management designates activities in which attempts are made to structure the totality of experiences in which the offender is immediately involved toward rehabilitative ends. . . . Environmental change refers to programs which try to effect alterations in some general, noninstitutional environment."[8]

Milieu management is best illustrated by the Highfields project described in chapter 4 and was used characteristically in institutions like Patuxent or in mental hospitals. Some criminologists stressed the value of such small therapeutic settings for successful treatment. Widespread implementation was a problem because most treatment programs existed

in large prisons with heterogeneous populations. Despite the trend toward classification and segregation of prisoners by type, very few correctional systems could afford to build the great number of prisons
needed to organize therapeutic communities, nor could they afford the
additional professional staff to work intensively with small groups. Although a few prisons attempted to isolate small groups of convicts in
milieu management experiments, the result in larger prisons was merely
some modifications in programs that did little to advance treatment.

One milieu management experiment attempted to solve the problem
of lack of staff by using convicts as therapists. In the early 1960s, the
California prison at Chino ran a group therapy program administered by
prisoner "social therapists." The administration chose a group of ten
prisoners to give intensive treatment to another group of convicts in an
isolated setting within the institution. Almost immediately, the ten therapists began to use their new role for illegal purposes and were subsequently fired. The success the program eventually enjoyed was small.

Some psychologists and criminologists still advocate such intensive behavioral change programs today.[9] The most notable example is that of
St. Elizabeth's Hospital for the Criminally Insane in Washington, D.C.
But these attempts are largely impractical because the staff time needed
to treat even one patient is so considerable that it is impossible to extend
the program to a meaningful number of prisoners.

The environmental change programs were more extensively used.
These included, of course, parole and probation but also work release,
halfway houses, and other community-oriented corrections endeavors.
One program that attempted to treat parolees (as well as correct incipient delinquents) was the Chicago Area Project, begun in the 1930s. It
had the following goals:

The Chicago Area Project operates on the assumption that much of the delinquency of slum areas is to be attributed to lack of neighborhood cohesiveness
and to the consequent lack of concern on the part of many residents about the
welfare of children. The Project strives to counteract this situation through en-
couraging local self-help enterprises through which a sense of neighborliness and
mutual responsibility will develop. It is expected that delinquency will decline as
youngsters become better integrated into community life and thereby influenced
by the values of conventional society rather than those of the underworld.[10]

Another effort at environmental change aimed at restructuring the social climate in slum areas was New York City's Mobilization for Youth
program of the early 1960s, which attempted to provide opportunities

for advancement in work, education, community, and group service. This program, like the Juvenile Delinquency and Control Act of 1961, was modeled on Cloward and Ohlin's theory of differential opportunity and was intended to provide slum children with the path to the bourgeoisie denied them by their present community culture. Most such programs did not meet with any great success in changing delinquent behavior patterns.[11] The continuing high crime rate in American slums and inner cities is evidence that the problem of crime is more complex than many of these criminologists think or want to think, and that solutions must affect the very structure of our society rather than offer small-scale "opportunities" for jobs and the like.

Be that as it may, treatment continued to be community oriented in the 1960s. Penologists finally realized the impossibility of rehabilitating anyone in the artificial setting of prison. The illogic of trying to treat convicts within the artificial environment of the "big house" was finally recognized in practice. Warden Harold Langlois of Rhode Island State Prison asked in 1966,

How do we handle what can be described as a cesspool of human inadequacy, degradation, misery, and immaturity? How do we program a social climate allowing for the presence—in total number—of people who are abnormal and negative in life? Why—it's simple, we confine them together, lock them up, put up a big wall and staff the facility with uniformed persons representing authority and call it a "correctional institution." We help it further by limiting visits, frustrating normal development of work and educational training programs, and placing in charge of this time bomb well-meaning but untrained persons in the field of behavioral sciences.[12]

Instead, criminologists used differential association principles to try to create programs that would eliminate the environmental factors that they believed created or advanced opportunities for criminal behavior. In practice, this meant preventing the "prisonization" process by placing the prisoner in a community instilled with "proper" middle-class values to "resocialize" him. Milieu management and environmental change methods such as work release and community corrections, as well as intensive parole and probation supervision, fit in well with the criminologists' principle of resocialization. Under controlled conditions, the prisoner was to learn proper bourgeois values through interpersonal relationships in a free community.

Resocialization was to be implemented after the convict was classified, placed in an institution, and treated and trained. He was then given the opportunity for off-grounds activities and paroled under supervision. Subsequently he was placed in off-grounds community corrections activities, such as work release, education release, camps, halfway houses, and prerelease centers.

Work release was a form of day parole, first introduced in 1913 in Wisconsin's Huber Law, which provided for daytime jobs for convicts in county jails. The practice did not become widespread until 1957, when North Carolina tried it for short-term misdemeanants. After receiving much favorable national publicity, the practice was extended to South Carolina and Maryland in the early 1960s, and by 1967 it had been adopted in about thirty states. Education release worked much the same way: it allowed convicts to enroll in educational programs not available in prisons. The problem with work and education release programs, however, was that they could only rarely be used for long-term felony offenders but only for misdemeanants, who did not pose a grave threat to the community in the first place.

The use of another off-grounds activity, the camp, became extensive in the late 1950s and 1960s. Camps could be road, farm, or forest camps. The programs relied largely on the honor of inmates and work instructors rather than on guards. But camps, too, were populated mainly by the least risky inmates. Some felony offenders could work their way down from maximum, medium and minimum security institutions to the honor camps before final release or parole. But coming from a maximum security prison could require several years of good behavior. The one undeniable asset of the camps was that they relieved the prevalent overcrowding of prisons and reduced idleness as well as segregating prisoners. (Because of the latter asset, some states, such as New York, called these institutions rehabilitation camps.)

Halfway houses were another type of honor system used for convicts. These were used primarily as intermediate custody institutions between prison and free society. Massachusetts, for instance, created halfway house dormitories for prisoners who were about to be paroled in order to train them for jobs and ease or "reintegrate" them back into the community. Many halfway houses allowed a convict greater control over his time than did work release or honor camp programs and therefore tested the resolve of the offender to go straight. Unfortunately, in many of these houses "freedom" meant the freedom to commit illegal acts, drink alcohol, or take drugs. The failures of halfway houses were glaring and widely publicized, and they completely overshadowed the successes. Consequently, few communities wished to have a halfway house located within their borders.

Furloughs were another form of community corrections. A supposedly minimum security risk convict could be released from prison on the condition that he return in seventy-two hours. In many cases, however, controls were lacking, and the furloughs were used for three-day binges and the like. Furloughs were usually granted for good behavior, but many prisoners in states with liberal furlough policies, such as California, began looking upon them as their right rather than as a reward for good behavior. When a furlough was denied, it caused great resentment and led to questioning the whole system. In addition, when furloughed convicts committed heinous crimes, the public outcry about "coddling criminals" further hurt the program. Furloughs were still being used in the 1980s; in the 1988 presidential campaign of Governor Michael Dukakis, a rape committed by a Massachusetts furloughed prisoner convicted of murder was brought up and blown out of proportion. Such publicity usually results in the curtailing or elimination of these programs. In fact, in August 1989, President George Bush moved to restrict the Federal Bureau of Prisons' Authority to furlough by excluding serious drug offenders and distributors, and those convicted of violent crimes.

As it had in the 1950s, California also led the way in instituting the correctional treatment programs of the 1960s. Commissioner of Corrections Richard McGee increased the use of forest and road camps and created three community corrections centers. All told, California ultimately had a total of three centers, thirty conservation camps, the Deuel Vocational Institution for difficult juveniles, Men's Colony West for older men, and the California Medical Facility for those with psychiatric disorders, besides traditional prisons such as San Quentin, Soledad, and Folsom.

McGee and his assistants also instituted treatment programs based on the typologies and other differential theories of the criminologists and penologists. Prisoners were treated according to levels of maturity, therapeutic milieus were attempted, and more and more prisoners were diverted from traditional institutions to probation, parole, and community centers. McGee instituted the Intensive Treatment Program at Chino that used convict "social therapists." He set up research units to evaluate treatment methods; the best known was the Pilot Intensive Counseling Organization, which studied inmates at the Deuel Vocational Institution. The convicts were divided into groups and given individual depth psychotherapy for an extended period of time. The results of this experiment were mixed and hardly conclusive. When certain convicts failed to become resocialized, the evaluators simply attributed it to the use of the wrong type of therapy.

California penologists also studied differential recidivism rates by giving immediate release to a control group of convicts and regular sentences to another group. They found that those who had been released earlier were less likely to return to crime; based solely on this evidence, California instituted a large probation-subsidy program to keep convicted felons out of jail. Other penologists, however, questioned the data and methodology used in this study and disputed its results. [13]

But the trend toward using group therapy, community corrections, differential typologies, and the like was overwhelming, and in 1965 even the federal government got into the act. James Bennett had pressed for the Indeterminate Sentence Act in 1958, and in 1965 he was able to secure the Prison Rehabilitation Act. This act authorized halfway houses, furloughs, and work release programs and put the Federal Bureau of Prisons in the mainstream of penology. Bennett also commissioned Daniel Glaser to study recidivism rates. Glaser's resulting book, *The Effectiveness of a Prison and Parole System,* which appeared in 1964, found that out of all convicts released in 1956, 31 percent had been reimprisoned by 1960. Other studies of particular states, such as California, showed even higher recidivism rates of 41 percent or more within three years of release. Although California led the way in the treatment model in the 1960s, it had one of the highest recidivism rates. The evidence for the success of the treatment model is obviously highly contradictory, and evaluative methods were not standardized.

California also had one of the highest imprisonment rates—the number of persons incarcerated rose from 65 per 100,000 population in 1944 to 145 in 1965. It did not take prisoners long to figure out just what the indeterminate sentence, along with therapeutic milieu and environmental change programs, meant in practice. Median time spent in California prisons rose from twenty-four months in 1959 to thirty-six in 1969, the longest prison terms in the country. [14]

Statistics show that approximately 70 percent of California convicts were on some form of probation or off-grounds activities during this period. Yet with only 30 percent actually incarcerated, the per capita imprisonment rate rose. What had happened in "progressive states" like California? A higher crime rate is one answer; but convicts also stayed in prison longer with the indeterminate sentence, which also helped incarceration rates to go up. Resistance to the indeterminate sentence emerged in the 1960s.

In 1962, a significant harbinger of change took place at the Lorton, Virginia, prison, the institution for Washington, D.C., offenders. Lorton's population had a majority of black prisoners. Throughout the late 1950s, the separatist Black Muslim organization had been working its way into prisons. This highly disciplined organization instilled a sense of worth and pride in blacks generally. Muslim leader Elijah Muhammed recognized the first Black Muslim prison group in San Quentin early in the 1960s, and the movement rapidly gained strength among blacks in penal institutions throughout the country. The cohesiveness of the Muslims and the new racial divisiveness engendered in prisons was not understood even by the more progressive wardens in the country. In 1962, the Lorton warden tried to suppress Black Muslim organizing, and his actions sparked a riot—the first with racial overtones.

In hindsight, it is not difficult to see that a storm in prison race relations was coming. Malcolm X put it well in his autobiography:

You let this caged-up black man start thinking, the same way I did when I first heard Elijah Muhammed's teachings, let him start thinking how with better breaks when he was young and ambitious he might have been a lawyer, a doctor, a scientist, anything. You let this caged-up black man start realizing, as I did, how from the first landing of the first slave ship, the millions of black men in America have been like sheep in a den of wolves. That's why black prisoners become Muslims so fast when Elijah Muhammed's teaching filters into their cages by way of other Muslim convicts. "The white man is the devil" is a perfect echo of that black convict's lifelong experience. [15]

The formation of Muslim and other separatist groups in prisons was a reflection of social forces in ferment outside prison walls. After the landmark 1954 Supreme Court decision *Brown vs. Board of Education,* the civil rights movement emerged in full force. Rising expectations among blacks and resistance to the civil rights movement by many whites wracked both the South and the North violently in the 1950s and 1960s. In 1966 it was stated before the National Advisory Committee on Civil Rights that "the masses of Negroes have not experienced tangible benefits in a significant way. This is so in education and housing. . . . Education of Negro masses for equal job opportunity programs have fallen far short of fulfillment." [16] The 1967 Kerner commission report explained that in the black inner cities, "segregation and poverty converge on the young to destroy opportunity and enhance failure. Crime, drug addiction, dependency on welfare, and bitterness and resentment against society . . . are the result." [17]

These social conditions and the assassination of Martin Luther King,

Jr., set off a wave of riots in the cities between 1964 and 1967. Not only were blacks rioting; those who were involved in the civil rights movement and the incipient anti–Vietnam War movement were getting more and more radicalized in their politics. In 1966 the Black Panthers organization was formed as a black separatist group and was soon active among black prisoners. The Panthers and similar groups were more prone to violence and Marxist politics than the Muslims were. Many of the white war protesters were also militant and Marxist. Criminologist Donald Cressey remarked that since "the prison . . . is a microcosm of the society in which it sits, militancy on the outside is bound to be reflected on the inside."[18] Free-society politics were making their way into the prisons, and the newly politicized prisoner began to blame a repressive society for his imprisonment, considering society the oppressor. He would not accept the label "deviant"; rather, he turned that idea on its head and called society deviant. It was society that needed to be treated under the medical model, not the prisoner. In short, he labeled himself a "political" prisoner rather than a "sick" one.

Compounding prison racial and political problems, the black population of penal institutions was rising precipitously. In the 1950s, the number of minority prisoners rose from 17,200 to 28,500; it dropped in the 1960s owing to the increased off-ground activities, but between 1950 and 1970 it rose from 30 percent to 40 percent. In many predominantly white states, prison populations had black majorities. The fact that blacks were incarcerated at greater rates than whites only reinforced black prisoners' belief that they were unjustly treated by society. Many in this population were eager to embrace the new militant political dogma that absolved them of blame for their criminal acts. In fact, they held themselves decriminalized.

With this, the prevailing liberal doctrine of bringing community values to prison for rehabilitative purposes turned on itself. Prison society accepted the values of free society just when many in the white middle class, upon whose values the penologists had modeled their reform techniques, were rejecting them. Many of the most vociferous and violent antiwar protesters hailed from the same white middle class that was supposed to provide normative values to delinquent subcultures. Many young whites rejected the world of their parents, "dropped out" of the middle class, took drugs, became hippies, left the country to avoid the draft, and committed other seemingly antisocial acts. Some ended up in prison for their activities and carried their political message with them. This was not the middle-class model for "differential opportunities" that had been envisioned by the criminologists. The free-society contradictions that penetrated the world of the prison, instead of helping prisoners adjust to their "sick" selves, made them reject the label and claim that prison was unjustly oppressive both to minority races and to the underclass. That is, the prisoners rejected the prison because they had finally accepted external community values.

Just at this time, the federal government decided that crime was a major social problem. The President of the United States appointed the commission on Law Enforcement and Administration of Justice, headed by James Vorenberg, to study the situation. The commission's Task Force on Corrections was dominated by California correctional officials and penologists. Among them were LaMar Emprey, director of the University of Southern California's Youth Studies Center and author of the book *Alternatives to Incarceration;* Richard McGee; Clarence Schrag of the University of Southern California; and Leslie Wilkins and Stuart Adams of the University of California at Berkeley. Other participants were Daniel Glaser, Austin MacCormick, Lloyd Ohlin, and Russell Oswald of New York (later a key actor at the infamous Attica riot).

With the task force staffed by people who had vested interest in the success of the New Penology, it is no wonder that its report strongly advocated treatment methods based on differential association and community organization. The report deplored the still-prevalent use of large maximum security prisons, with their brutality, idleness, and understaffing. It repeated statements of years before on the fortress prisons:

There are today 400 institutions for adult felons in the country, ranging from some of the oldest and largest prisons in the world to forestry camps for 30 or 40 trusted inmates. Some are grossly understaffed and underequipped. . . . Overcrowding and idleness are the salient features of some, brutality and corruption of a few others. . . . There are still many large maximum-security prisons operating in the United States today. The directory of the American Correctional Association showed a 1965 average population of over 2,000 inmates in 21 prisons. Four of these had well over 4,000 inmates each: San Quentin in California; the Illinois State Prison complex at Joliet and Stateville; the Michigan State Prison at Jackson; and the Ohio State Penitentiary at Columbus.[19]

The task force's report read like a précis of the writings of the New Penologists of earlier decades.

The general underlying premise for the new directions in corrections is that crime and delinquency are symptoms of failures and disorganization of the community as well as of individual offenders. In particular, these failures are seen as depriving offenders of contact with the institutions that are basically responsible for assuring development of law-abiding conduct: sound family life, good schools, employment, recreational opportunities, and desirable companions, to name only some of the more direct influences. The substitution of deleterious habits, standards, and associates for these strengthening influences contributes to crime and delinquency.

The task of corrections therefore includes building or rebuilding solid ties between offender and community, integrating or reintegrating the offender into community life—restoring family ties, obtaining employment and education, securing in the larger sense a place for the offender in the routine functioning of society. This requires not only efforts directed toward changing the individual offender, which has been almost the exclusive focus of rehabilitation, but also mobilization and change of the community and its institutions.[20]

The report drew analogies between treatment in corrections and treatment in mental health and in even education; it proposed the solutions offered by the theories based on community organization and reintegration and on the instillation of proper middle-class values through increased opportunities. The task force paid tribute to Sutherland's theory of differential association and relied heavily on Cloward and Ohlin's influential *Delinquency and Opportunity*.

Perhaps the development of these concepts most pertinent to reintegration as a mode of correctional treatment is that of Cloward and Ohlin which built on work by [Albert] Cohen [*Delinquent Boys: The Culture of the Gang*] and others. It asserts that much delinquency is the result of inability to gain access to legitimate opportunities in our society, coupled with availability of illegitimate opportunities that are seized as alternatives by frustrated persons. Corrective action therefore should seek to increase the opportunities of the offender to succeed in law-abiding activities, while reducing his contacts with the criminal world.[21]

The task force strongly recommended community corrections centers to implement the reintegration process. Community corrections centers, unlike the traditional maximum security prisons, would be small, informal, and located near population centers. In the halfway house and juvenile correctional center, the task force recommended that differential treatment be used: "This type of institution would perform many functions. It would receive newly committed inmates and carry out extensive screening and classification with them. For those who are not returned quickly to community treatment, the new institutions would provide short-term intensive treatment before placing them in the community under appropriate supervision."[22]

The thrust of the report was to advocate reintegrating the convict into the community and dealing with his problems in his social context. The framers of the study saw these methods as soundly based on social science theory and as avoiding institutional isolation and the labeling effect.

The task force pointed to the disparity between the proportion of prisoners in community corrections and the proportion of prison personnel employed in community corrections. In 1965, more than half of all convicts were on probation, 684,088 out of 1,282,386. If parolees were included, 67 percent of all offenders were in some type of community corrections program. There were 121,000 people employed in corrections, but of them, only 15 percent were in community corrections; 85 percent were in institutions to guard or treat 33 percent of all offenders. Only 20 percent of staff were even marginally involved in treatment functions, while the remainder had administrative or custodial responsibilities. In addition, 20 percent of the nation's correctional budget was going for community corrections, while 80 percent went to penal institutions.

The task force recognized that very few of the treatment programs called for over the years had been implemented and that there was little communication between institutions, jurisdictions, and programs. James Vorenberg, in an article separate from the report, lamented that this isolation has contributed in corrections to the tendency to faddishness in rehabilitative programming—the rush to try a method that seems new and hopeful but that may have failed elsewhere, the rejection of a program that appears to have failed but with slight modifications may have succeeded in another jurisdiction. It has meant that some agencies have made great strides in reducing recidivism while others have remained backwaters, grossly understaffed, little interested in imaginative innovation, and unstimulated by contact with more progressive counterparts.[23]

The commission's report touched on a salient point that, with racial tensions and the new politicization of prisoners, would become increasingly important in the following years.

It is perhaps ironic that trends in modern corrections toward more humane treatment and greater emphasis on rehabilitation and community supervision have increasingly raised issues of fair process and the rights of offenders. . . . Changes in correctional philosophy have encouraged this concern for the rights of offenders. As long as the dominant purpose of corrections was punishment, the treatment of offenders could be and was regarded in law as a matter of grace in which offenders had few rights. But when decisions are made with the object of helping offenders, and when moreover they purport to have some rational or even scientific basis, it becomes anomalous to regard them as unreviewable matters of grace. [24]

From the beginning of the U.S. penitentiary system, the judicial system had basically ignored lawsuits that challenged the internal operation of prisons. Social control was the primary ideological reason for this policy; judges reasoned that interfering in prison routines would undermine discipline and cause hazardous conditions for staff and convicts alike. Other ostensible reasons were "separation of powers" and "lack of judicial expertise." [25] Under this "hands-off policy," prison officials were allowed to run their institutions as they pleased.

But the activism of the civil rights movement and the politicization of prisoners put an end to this policy. The judicial system began not only to hear such suits but to rule in favor of prisoners. Early convict victories were in the area of freedom of religion for Black Muslims and other religious groups. In its 1961 decision on *Monroe v. Pape,* the U.S. Supreme Court resurrected the Civil Rights Act of 1871, which enabled blacks to sue on constitutional issues directly in federal courts, thus bypassing prejudiced state courts. This led lawyers to test the constitutional rights of prisoners, among other things. In 1964 in *Cooper v. Pate,* the Court allowed prisoners to sue state officials in federal court for the first time. Federal judges also began to protect the legal rights of prisoners. These rulings were only the beginning of the swarm of litigation in which prisoners would be involved in the 1970s.

Because the Eighth Amendment to the U.S. Constitution prohibits cruel and unusual punishment, convicts' attorneys succeeded in forcing prisons to abandon all forms of corporal punishment and in prohibiting deplorable prison living conditions. Prisoners won the right to unimpeded access to the courts, and restrictions on legal correspondence were ruled illegal. Prisons were forbidden to punish convicts who sued or criticized prison administrations. In 1969 the Supreme Court ruling in *Johnson v. Avery* allowed jailhouse lawyers to help prisoners who could not afford to hire lawyers for their cases. [26]

These court decisions emboldened the prisoners to take further measures, but they also caused a smoldering resentment among prison officials. The latter were no longer obeyed or given any respect solely because of their positions. In their minds, they had been stripped of such respect by the courts. Their attitude, coupled with the new prison activism, set the stage for riots and reaction.

Politically aware prisoners in the 1960s, helped by liberal and radical lawyers, took actions of rebellion, riot, and defiance of authority that changed the very nature of prison revolt. Most telling was the race riot at San Quentin in 1967. A minor incident sparked this riot: A guard put his finger in a black convict's glass of milk. When the prisoner complained, he was surrounded by guards intent on beating him. Other prisoners pressed in on the guards, and they eventually retreated and locked up the complaining convict. The next day, two convict kitchen workers were fired when they were caught signing a petition that demanded his release. Talk began that there would be a general strike of black prisoners if the convict were not released by the following Sunday. He was not. On Monday the blacks struck. To show that the action was racially unified, they did not ask the whites or Hispanics to join them.

It was a very foggy day, and visibility was difficult on the yard. A few fights broke out when some convicts went to work. In one of these fights, a white convict was killed. The next day, as the black strike continued, whites prepared for a fight. The prison administration, almost certainly aware of the situation, made no attempt to clear the yard or to lock down the institution. Apparently, white guards prodded white convicts with remarks such as "I know you guys aren't going to let the niggers get away with it."[27]

On Wednesday, warfare broke out in the vast San Quentin yard. The guards fired their weapons from above on the guard rails and eventually herded the convicts back into their cells. There many were beaten.

Almost two thousand inmates were involved in the San Quentin altercation. When it was over, the more aware convicts of all ethnicities realized that racial strife was self-destructive and attempted reconciliation and a unified front against prison authorities. They were so successful that in 1968 they staged a general strike that brought the prison to a near standstill. Prison officials broke it up by transferring the leaders. But later in the year, the convicts staged a Unity Day that resulted in a legislative committee investigation of their grievances. The unified front did not last, however, and before long racial strife broke out again.

What is important is that such a strike was unheard of twenty years earlier. Prison officials knew how to handle traditional riots, but this strange new political activism and unity on the part of the caged was something new. It frightened even the New Penologists, and many rethought and eventually abandoned their deeply held principles. Prison radicals pushed many treatment-minded penologists over to the custody side. Along the way, confidence in the rehabilitative process was lost. The rationale for treatment differentials was undermined, and the whole idea of rehabilitation became indefensible.[28]

Something was clearly wrong with the nation's correctional system, and not even the most die-hard progressive could deny it. The thirty-nine riots in 1969 and the fifty-nine in 1970 were enough to convince just about everyone of the continuing failure of the system.[29] A series of studies on treatment programs beginning in the 1960s also threw doubt on the whole idea of rehabilitation. Two in California and one in New York asserted that group therapy and other treatment methods had little effect on recidivism rates.[30]

In the 1970s, the treatment model came under attack by both penologists and custodians. The ideological foundation of the prison system since its beginning was eroding, and there was little to replace it. The early 1970s saw further politicization of the prison and an increase in violence and riots. New schools of criminology attacked correctional methods from all sides, while those who still clung forlornly to outmoded treatment methods were swept away.

Chapter Six

Violence and Revolt: The 1970s

Scribbled on a prison wall after the Attica riot of 1971 was an inmate's ATTICA FELL 9–9–71—FUCK YOU PIG! Beneath it, a state policeman wrote, RETAKEN ON 9-13-71—31 DEAD NIGGERS.[1] Telling of violence and eventual defeat, these graffiti sum up the prison movement in the 1970s.

The San Quentin Unity Day strike in August 1968 was a harbinger of things to come, but at the time prison officials did not fully grasp the changing direction of the prison movement. The social forces of the 1960s radicalized many segments of the population, including both convicts and penal theorists, who took on the prison bureaucracy and old guard. An article in 1968 in the San Quentin underground newspaper *The Outlaw* warned of the need for a unified front between the races: "Some of us cons don't seem to know which side we're on. We're obsessed with nearsighted disputes based on race, ideology, group identity, and so on. We expend our energies despising and distrusting each other. Don't be so critical of the other races. All of this is helping the California Department of Corrections. We permit them to keep us at each others' throats. But a handful of us are calling for unity. This is for a purpose. We want to crush this empire that has been built upon our suffering."[2]

Corrections leaders and administrators did not take seriously the radicals' and prisoners' calls for unity against them, the common oppressor. But at the beginning of the new decade, the American prison system experienced cataclysmic shock: prisoners were moving from unity movements to insurrection. Convict solidarity actions, along with both radical and moderate penological theories, would help kill the medical model of treatment and usher in a new age of repression.

The first significant event to set the tone for the 1970s occurred at Soledad Prison in California. O-wing—the "adjustment unit" of the institution—contained 108 dark, six-by-nine-foot cells that had little ventilation, no lights, and only a circular hole for a toilet. In the 1960s, O-wing had been the subject of a prisoners' federal suit that had charged that conditions in the unit were so deplorable that they constituted "cruel and unusual punishment" under the Constitution. The federal district court in San Francisco heard the case, and in 1966 the presiding judge concluded:

When, as it appears in the case at the bar, the responsible prison authorities in the case of the strip cells have abandoned elemental concepts of decency by permitting conditions of a shocking and debased nature, then the courts must intervene—and intervene promptly—to restore the primal rules of a civilized community in accord with the mandate of the United States Constitution.

In the opinion of the Court, the type of confinement in the foregoing summary of the inmate's testimony results in a slow burning fire of resentment on the part of the inmates until it finally explodes in open revolt. Requiring man or beast to live, eat and sleep under degrading conditions pointed out in the testimony creates a condition that inevitably does violence to elemental concepts of decency.[3]

The decision provided a measure of satisfaction to the prisoners and brought conditions at Soledad to public attention, but few practical improvements resulted. The court could not break entirely with the traditional "hands-off" policy of not interfering in bureaucrats' running of prisons, and therefore it did not mandate the implementation of specific procedures by which the correctional system was to comply with the Constitution.

In 1968 a black convict was stabbed and killed in the outdoor yard at Soledad, and the yard closed for two years after. During that time, in the absence of the open yard, prisoners were let out for only thirty minutes a day for exercise on the cell tiers. Racial animosities at the prison (some provoked by guards) had been at a fever pitch ever since the killing, resulting in repeated stabbings and killings; both whites and blacks lived in mutual fear of race war.

Early in 1970 the administration reopened the yard with a directive whose wording almost dared the convicts to come out of their cells and into a contentious situation on the yard: "Failure to prepare for yard release will be considered refusal to exercise, and will result in the inmate's exercise for that period being cancelled." Why the yard was reopened at

the height of racial tensions is open to conjecture, but subsequent occur-
rences in the yard lead one to believe that if the officials were not delib-
erately fomenting racial strife, they were certainly doing nothing to
prevent it.

On 13 January 1970, seven black convicts were let out to Soledad's O-
wing exercise yard. Among them was one W. L. Dolen, who in 1969 had
brought suit against the Soledad warden for fomenting an extremely dangerous racist atmosphere in the prison. Eight white convicts, most of
whom had previously participated in racial fights, were also let out of
their cells and joined the blacks in the yard. None of the convicts were
armed as they entered the yard, but because of the earlier killings of the
two black convicts, apparently everyone expected a retaliatory fight. Almost immediately Nolen punched one of the whites, and a melee began.
The gun-tower guard opened fire on the brawlers and killed Nolen and
two other blacks. For a guard to fire directly on convicts when he himself
was in no personal danger went against all standard procedure and was
never sufficiently explained, yet three days later a coroner's jury found
the killings justified. This action set off a two-year period of violence
between (mostly black) prisoners and guards.

On 16 January, John Mills, a relief guard in Y-wing of the prison, was
beaten and thrown off the third tier of the wing. He was the first—but
not the last—guard killed at Soledad. In July, a convict murdered another
guard. Five more murders of guards followed in the next two years.

George Jackson was a black inmate who had originally been convicted
of a seventy-dollar theft and given a short term; he had nonetheless
served eleven years for a variety of prison offenses. Jackson had been
involved in much of the racial strife of the 1960s and had converted to
Marxist-Leninism through his readings of Malcolm X and other radical
thinkers. He had organized a Marxist study group in prison and had attempted to allay divisions between the races at Soledad.

Jackson was charged, along with two other blacks, with the murder of
John Mills. (Ten black convicts in all were eventually indicted for the
crime.) When the news of Jackson's charge became known, sympathetic
groups in the San Francisco Bay area organized what was called the
Soledad Brothers Defense Fund. The actions of these groups, including
their investigations into the charges against the three, caused the prison
management to transfer Jackson to San Quentin.

Jackson's younger brother Jonathan was apparently embittered at the
court's treatment of his brother. He raided the Marin County courthouse

on 7 August 1970, took hostages (including a judge who was trying another case), and demanded the release of his brother. In the ensuing
shoot-out Jonathan, the judge, and two others were killed.

The Soledad Brothers' case fueled the new prison movement. In August 1970 the Marin County Superior Court planned for the sake of
safety to hold its sessions on the Soledad case in San Quentin. The prisoners, fearing an administrative setup concerning the charges, protested
by staging a sit-down strike in the yard. Led by Black Panthers, they
presented a list of demands to prison officials.

> That all political prisoners be freed.
>
> That the Soledad Three be freed.
>
> That a black warden be hired.
>
> That a black associate warden of custody be hired.
>
> That a black associate warden of care and treatment be hired.
>
> That a Mexican warden be hired.
>
> That a Mexican associate warden of custody be hired.
>
> That a Mexican associate warden of care and treatment be hired.
>
> That nonwhite prisoners have proportional representation in all ad-
> ministrative, industrial, and vocational positions in the prison.
>
> That B Section and A Section be closed until they are made to conform
> to sanitary and health standards.
>
> That men in B Section, A Section, and the adjustment center be given
> one full hour of exercise a day and be given the rights that other
> prisoners have.
>
> That all men presently condemned to death be given political asylum
> abroad.
>
> That all forms of capital punishment and mass genocide on the people
> by the brutal hands of the American bureaucracies immediately
> cease by order of the Free World Solidarity Revolutionary Army for
> the People.
>
> That all prisoners being tried by the Superior Court within the walls
> of San Quentin be tried by their peers.[4]

Approximately eight hundred convicts, or 25 percent of the prison
population, participated in the sit-down strike. The leader, Warren Wells,
attempted to ensure that participation in the sit-down was interracial and
called for "Blue Power" after the blue clothing that California prisoners

wore. Wells's call was yet another manifestation of solidarity based on prisonhood rather than race. One San Quentin prisoner remarked, "Naturally, when you are put here and you've never lived with blacks before, you don't like them. But in the past couple of years people have begun to realize that you have to work together."[5] The preamble to the above demands read, "Yes, they'll probably break the strike but the seed has been planted again and it'll grow, for many Convicts are realizing that the cause is Right, that the taking of Human Rights & Slavery were abolished many, many years ago. If you can't see the light, stay in the darkness where you'll not be seen or heard. Black, White, Brown Convicts, Blue Power, the saying is, 'We shall overcome,' by peacefully being slaves no longer & peaceful is until it's not Suicide and there's no other way."

Despite the rhetoric of class unity, prison officials succeeded in breaking the strike partially by using racist tactics to turn it into a racial conflict. White guards taunted white prisoners with remarks such as "The niggers sure ran a game on you."[6] Prison officials attempted to discredit the list of demands by calling them ridiculous, asinine, and the like. In truth, many of the demands were unrealistic and beyond the power of the administration to give. But the importance of the strike is that it reflected a qualitative change in prisoners' attitudes toward their incarceration and in the very nature of their prison existence. It was almost an epistemological break between acceptance of the Progressive era's idea of the criminal as sick and treatable and acceptance of the classical notion of the moral autonomy of the societal offender. This change rightfully caused great fear in the hearts of correctional officials because, if left unchecked, it could transform the rules of the whole game.

In the aftermath of the sit-down strike in 1971, a guard at San Quentin shot and killed George Jackson after he and some companions seized the "adjustment center."

Another manifestation of the new attitudes occurred at the Long Island, New York, branch of the Queens House of Detention in October 1970 when convicts rioted, took hostages, and issued a set of demands. Many of their demands were related to racist issues and had been inspired by the Black Panthers. Police eventually stormed the jail and crushed the riot.

A month later, approximately two thousand convicts (out of 2,400) at Folsom Prison in California staged the longest nonviolent strike in prison history to date. For some time before the strike, the prisoners had been attempting to forge a spirit of interracial cooperation and form a convict labor movement. As hard as prison officials tried, they could not break the momentum of the convicts' efforts. On 3 November 1970 the prisoners stopped work in unison and stayed in their cells for nineteen days, despite constant pressure from the prison administration to go back to the daily routine. The Folsom prisoners issued a manifesto with thirty-one demands; the preamble sums up well the spirit of the strike as well as the changing attitudes of the prisoners.

Brothers and Sisters,

This list of demands comes from our brothers at Folsom Prison—Black, Brown, Red, Yellow, and White. They believe that now is the time *to determine the direction of their own lives* [emphasis added], and to stop letting themselves be the Pawns of the Adult Authority and the California Department of Corrections. Their struggle is your struggle. The walls that wall our brothers in wall us out. Consider how these demands affect all of our lives. To continue their effort and to make these demands STATEWIDE, they need our utmost support.

ALL POWER TO THE PEOPLE!

This preamble explicitly states the radical prisoner's claim to Kantian moral autonomy, with personal responsibility for both the crime and the punishment. This was an abrupt change from the treatment philosophy and utilitarian ethics that had prevailed for almost a century, and it represented a new radicalism.

Many of the thirty-one Folsom demands related to deplorable living and working conditions, the importance of legal rights, the racism of the officials, the violence of the guards, the need for vocational programs, and the like. But more important, a few attacked the crux of the Progressive penal system. The tenth demand called for "the passing of a minimum and maximum term bill which calls for an end to indeterminate sentences whereby a man can be warehoused indefinitely, rehabilitated or not." The twenty-third demand called for the abolition of the Adult Authority and the installation of a popularly elected parole board in its place. It succinctly summed up objections to the practice of parole: "In a world where many crimes are punished by indeterminate sentences; where authority acts within secrecy and within vast discretion, and gives heavy weight to accusations by prison employees against inmates, inmates feel trapped unless they are willing to abandon their desire to be independent men." The cry for independence, autonomy, and hence moral responsibility for societal transgressions is repeated. (Twenty-nine of these same demands were made by the rioters at Attica.)

Throughout the Folsom strike, prison officials refused to negotiate or even to recognize the united effort of the convicts. After nineteen days, the administration broke the strike with a combination of brute force and trickery. As one convict recalled,

The strike was broken *not* because the prisoners had become disenchanted. The Collective Spirit and optimism were too real to make me believe that the prisoners went to work as a result of disillusionment. . . . Therefore it is only logical that devious means were employed to break the strike.

It is clear as crystal that [the warden] used political deception and brute force to get the prisoners to go back to work. On the 23rd of November the prison pigs, armed with rifles and wooden clubs, stopped in front of each man's cell and ordered each man back to work. Of course the order was weighted down with the threat of violence. Not wanting to be shot or clubbed to death, the prisoner naturally complied with the pigs' vicious method of brute force.

Apparently the administration circulated leaflets with misinformation that created conflict between the strikers under the convicts' names, which helped get the kitchen workers back in order to make hot meals. Once the kitchen was staffed, unity broke down.

Although the Folsom strike was broken, the prisoners' unity movement continued at other prisons throughout the country. Significantly, the call for convict power—that is, for autonomy and self-determination—was common to the movement. Although the most vocal and active prisoners and ex-convicts working for unity and making demands were in the minority nationwide, they did set the tone and provide the impetus for action. Similarly, in free society, the minority of the young population who were antiwar activists eventually wielded the most political influence in the course of the conflict.

Just as the nonviolent civil rights and antiwar movements broke off into groups advocating new, often violent methods, the prisoners' movement that started out with sit-down strikes erupted in the bloodbath of Attica.

In May 1971 at Attica Correctional Institution in New York, several prisoners—including radical whites, Muslims, Panthers, and Young Lords (a Puerto Rican group)—formed the Attica Liberation Faction. They issued twenty-nine demands, including the right to organize and an end to the present parole system.[7] The newly appointed state commissioner of corrections, Russell Oswald, acknowledged the demands and promised to discuss them further. He corresponded with the faction leaders. He was earnestly concerned with widespread reform of the prison system. But subsequent events happened quickly, and Oswald could not handle the exploding situation. He did not visit the prison, as he had promised he would. News of the killing of George Jackson at San Quentin on 21 August had a chilling effect on prisoners and officials alike. Tension filled the penitentiary, and everyone knew that eventually something would happen.

On 2 September, Oswald visited the prison briefly, but family matters soon called him away. One convict complained, "People [were] hollering, 'That's a cop-out . . .' because he didn't do nothing. . . . He didn't so much as make one concession, such as giving a man soap or giving a man a extra shower. He did not make any concessions whatsoever."[8]

On 8 September, a guard attempted to discipline two convicts who were apparently fighting in the yard; one of the prisoners pushed the guard, and an obstreperous crowd assembled. Officials were able to disperse the crowd without violence, and a Lieutenant Curtiss promised the prisoners that there would be no repercussions because of the incident.

But that evening, guards appeared at the cells of two of the prisoners who had been most vocal during the disturbance and took them away to the adjustment center. Convicts witnessing the removal protested with such cries as "Wait until tomorrow, we're gonna tear this joint up."[9] The next morning, tension and resentment were at their height. When Curtiss (who actually had had nothing to do with the disciplinary action the night before) attempted to lead the convicts back to their cells after breakfast, the prisoners beat him. They then captured several guards, got the keys to open the yard gates, and took control of the intersection called "Times Square" that gave access to most of the cell blocks. Within a short time, the rioters were in control of the interior of the prison. They started fires, broke out weapons, and took blow torches and other equipment from the shop.

The administration was unprepared to handle a large-scale disturbance; it had a personnel shortage, an antiquated communications system, and no viable riot plan. One officer admitted that "there had been a riot plan of sorts, which all supervisory officers were to familiarize themselves with, but it pertained largely to a single area, an isolated area where a disturbance might occur. It didn't provide for an institution-wide problem."[10] Within twenty minutes of the outbreak, the convicts had seized the four main cell blocks, the surrounding areas, and forty-three guards and prison employees as hostages. An estimated three-fifths of Attica's 2,243 convicts participated in the uprising, and approximately 75 percent of them were black or Puerto Rican. This was no mere riot; it was a veritable insurrection.

For much of the day, convicts roamed the yard and raided the commissary in a party atmosphere. But when the hostages were brought across the yard, the mood turned nasty, and some of the convicts attacked them. The Muslims took a leadership role in protecting the hostages from those seeking revenge; they were joined by some Panther, Young Lord, and white leaders. The factions eventually compromised, tensions lifted, and a common front emerged. The convicts formed committees and prepared for a siege. They issued a set of demands that highlighted the political character of the uprising. One of the leaders, L. D. Barkley, took a bullhorn and read the following demands, addressed to Governor Nelson Rockefeller and President Richard Nixon:

We want Complete Amnesty, Meaning freedom for all and from all physical, mental and legal reprisals.

We want now speedy and safe transportation out of confinement, to a Non-Imperialistic country.

We demand that Fed. Government intervine, so that we will be under direct Fed. Jurisdiction.

We demand the reconstruction of Attica Prison to be done by Inmates and/or inmates supervision.

We intensely demand that all Communication will be conducted in "OUR" Domain "GUARANTEEING SAFE TRANSPORTATION TO AND FROM."

The sixth demand was for negotiations through several people who were believed to be sympathetic to the prisoners: attorney William Kunstler, newspaperman Tom Wicker, Assemblyman Arthur O. Eve, and representatives from the Panthers, the Fortune Society, and other radical and prison reform groups.

Commissioner Oswald agreed to negotiate. His action went against standard procedure concerning hostages, which called for retaking the prison without regard for hostages, to discourage subsequent taking of hostages. Oswald did otherwise, and against the advice of his aides, he conducted negotiations through the civilian observers, admitted the press, and even made some concessions.

Two civilians played important roles in the early stages of the negotiations: Herman Schwartz, a lawyer who specialized in prisoners' rights, and black Buffalo Assemblyman Arthur Eve, who had been active in prison reform. Both men persuaded Oswald to allow them into the yard to talk to the convict leaders. The convicts gave Schwartz their list of immediate demands; the lawyer saw that most of the demands were impractical and convinced them to supplement the list with some practical demands.

The Attica insurrectionists copied their practical demands primarily from the Folsom strike manifesto, which addressed prison living conditions, censorship, work conditions, food, education, medical care, religious freedom, the right to organize in political groups, and of course the parole system. The inmates also demanded a federal injunction against reprisals. Schwartz had told them that they could not obtain criminal amnesty for actions they committed during the uprising, but they could get an injunction barring the prison administration from making physical or other reprisals.

Schwartz obtained the injunction. But he brought it to the convicts without a seal, and they became wary and refused to accept it. As one of the leaders said, "This injunction is garbage. It doesn't give us criminal amnesty, it's limited to one day, and it doesn't have a seal."[11] No matter how much Schwartz tried to explain and convince them, the convicts thought they were being tricked, and more mistrust entered the negotiations.

Dialogue continued through the following days. The committee of outsiders grew to an unmanageable thirty members. Eventually this was whittled to an executive committee of six, which worked out a package of thirty-three proposals that the committee thought both the state and the convicts would accept. Commissioner Oswald did accept twenty-eight of them, even though many were vaguely worded and lacked specificity. One of the proposals that he did not accept was amnesty, which put off the convict negotiators and then mistrust grew further. (It is interesting to note that both the outsiders' proposals and Oswald's response contained a proposal to "institute realistic, effective rehabilitation programs for all inmates according to their offense and personal needs." The old rhetoric dies slowly.)

Meanwhile, one of the officers who had been hurt in the initial takeover died. His death meant that the issue of amnesty became of primary importance partly because without amnesty many lifers would face the death sentence under New York's capital punishment statutes. The convicts believed that all of them could be charged with conspiracy to murder.

After this development, tension mounted on both sides. State and other police had been gathering in force ever since the initial seizure; they too were deeply affected by the news of the officer's death. The outside observers felt it was time for Governor Rockefeller to come to Attica. One of the governor's aides told him that amnesty, asylum, and removal of the superintendent were the real issues. The governor decided not to come and refused to grant amnesty on principle, even if he had had the constitutional authority to grant it. He proposed to accept many of the other inmate demands and was prepared to implement them. However, because he refused to grant amnesty—which was first and foremost in the convicts' minds—they rejected his proposals immediately. Furthermore, the outside negotiators were forbidden by the administration to reenter the yard. The impasse became obvious, and the police readied for an assault.

It is difficult to say what would have happened if Rockefeller had come to Attica. The official commission investigating the uprising criticized the governor for staying away.

No one can be sure whether the Governor's presence would have succeeded in producing a settlement that had eluded Oswald and the observers. Present or not, the Governor was unwilling to grant amnesty, the critical inmate demand. . . . The Commission nevertheless believes that conditions made it appropriate for the Governor to go to Attica. At the time of the uprising, the Governor realized that the prison system had long been neglected and was in need of major reform. Many of the inmates' grievances were acknowledged to be legitimate by both the Commissioner and the Governor. . . . It is possible that, even without the grant of amnesty, the Governor's presence at Attica would have overcome inmate mistrust of the state's commitment to reform, and induced acceptance of the 28 points. Some inmates have expressed this view to the commission.["12]

The convicts became increasingly combative and violent. As Dr. Warren Hanson, the surgeon who treated the convicts and hostages during the revolt, described the situation, "I went back up to the Commissioner's office and told them . . . that there was sort of a psychological deterioration taking place. There seemed to be a battle for control . . . [and] it seemed to me that the violent forces were gaining more and more control over the conservatives."[13]

Some convicts were forced to build trenches, rapes occurred, and three were beaten and stabbed to death. One convict later observed, "People were getting restless, you know. The food was low. Everyone was getting short-tempered with each other more or less, and it was just a matter of tension just building up, waiting, waiting, waiting, waiting, wondering what the outcome would be."[14]

After four days, conditions deteriorated on all sides. The governor viewed the matter as an insurrection against the authority of the state, and not a mere riot; he was correct. He believed that rebellion had to be put down with force. Finally, on Sunday night Oswald decided that the police and guards would assault the prison if the convicts did not accept the proposals and release the hostages by the next morning. When the prisoners did neither, Oswald, as the official in charge, made the final decision to assault the prison, with the governor's approval.

Although restraint was officially mandated, the national guard and the state troopers let off a frightful barrage of gunpower. It was all over in four minutes: Thirty-nine people had been killed, and eighty-eight others wounded. The police killed nine hostages as well as many of the convict negotiators. The commission later said of the slaughter, "With the exception of Indian massacres in the late 19th century, the State Police assault which ended the four-day prison uprising was the bloodiest one-day encounter between Americans since the Civil War."

Once the prison was retaken, the physical reprisals against the convicts began with vicious vengeance. Guards and police beat, kicked, and verbally abused convicts in the immediate days after the retaking. The administration took no action to prevent vengeance on the convicts; in fact, officials seemed to condone and then cover up the brutality inflicted on the prisoners.

Attica became the symbol of prison brutality and oppression. The underlying, always present, retributive character of the penal system was finally out in the open, and the era of treatment was dead.

To some prison activists, the incidents at Soledad, Attica, and other prisons marked the beginning of a revolutionary movement that would eventually overthrow the whole antiquated carceral network. In a sense they were right; a revolution was occurring, but the new age was not necessarily one to their liking.

Many of these activists responded with enthusiasm to the new prisoners' movement. To them, reform meant not only the traditional demands for decent food, living conditions, and the like, but a brand-new ideology and an overhauling not only of the prison system but of society at large. Like some radical activists in free society in the 1970s, prison activists advocated a form of socialism with an analysis that cut across racial lines and was based primarily on class consciousness. They called for greater education—that is, for reading "the sophisticated political writings of past and present revolutionaries." These activists sought to ally themselves with radical Third World groups, as well as with the new, younger breed of revolutionists of the late 1960s and early 1970s.

These activists were quite right in emphasizing the similarities between prison protests and free society protests. Many criminologists and penologists picked up their standard and formed the Marxist and critical schools of criminology. These two schools tended to overlap; the major difference between them was the Marxist school's emphasis on *praxis* or activism as opposed to purely theoretical studies. Both schools' principles fit neatly into the prison activists' call for revolution. One leading advocate of Marxist and critical criminology, Richard Quinney, stated the principles of these schools in his *Critique of Legal Order.*

American society is based on an advanced capitalist economy.

The state is organized to serve the interests of the dominant economic class, the capitalist ruling class.

Criminal law is an instrument of the state and ruling class to maintain and perpetuate the existing social and economic order.

Crime control in capitalist society is accomplished through a variety of institutions and agencies established and administered by a government elite, representing ruling class interests, for the purpose of establishing domestic order.

The contradictions of advanced capitalism—the disjunction between existence and essence—require that the subordinate classes remain oppressed by whatever means necessary, especially through the coercion and violence of the legal system.

Only with the collapse of capitalist society and the creation of a new society, based on socialist principles, will there be a solution to the crime problem.[15]

In his *Class, State, and Crime,* Quinney wrote that prisons are primarily instruments of social control to contain the surplus population of the working class. He argued that during the transition from a bourgeois state to a socialist one, what he calls *popular justice* will replace criminal justice—meaning that people will work out their problems collectively outside the legal institutions of the capitalist class. His hope was that with the coming of socialism, popular justice will "become institutionalized into the society and the state." Popular justice will then protect the working class from class enemies and elitist tendencies. By logical extension, once popular justice becomes part of the state apparatus and communism replaces bourgeois society, the surplus population problem is resolved and the rational for prisons vanishes. In short, as David Gordon observed about radical criminology, "Nearly all crimes in capitalist societies represent perfectly rational responses to . . . the organization of capitalist institutions, for those crimes help provide a means to survival in a society within which survival is never assured."[16]

It is easy to understand why such orthodox Marxist ideas appealed to the radical prison activists of the 1970s: Capitalism causes crime, and the opponents of the capitalist system are thrown in the prisons. Abolish capitalism, and you will abolish crime and hence prisons. But however appealing or true this theory was, utopia still had to be attained. Until it was, under all governments no matter what their form (including transitional socialism), enemies of the state would still exist and they would still have to be incarcerated in some way.

Many radical penologists gave little thought to the practical implications of their theories—that is, to prison conditions during the transitional periods. The belief that capitalism must be destroyed did not improve the contemporary prison environments that convicts had to endure daily. In practice, the radicalization of prison populations brought about a harsher repression of convicts. According to some of the more popular social theorists of the day, such as Herbert Marcuse, this repression was only mirroring repression in free society, and the more repression there was, the more likely it was that the revolution would come.

The fact was that after Soledad, Folsom, and Attica, more and more convicts *did* feel a deeper and stronger class consciousness and did become more politicized. All evidence indicates that to fight back, prison officials provoked racial and other incidents among convicts that resulted in a variety of fights behind the bars. In California, for instance, San Quentin experienced four stabbings in one day, and violence increased throughout the system in the three years after the incidents at Soledad and Attica and George Jackson's killing. When a guard was killed at California's Deuel Vocational Institution, the commissioner of corrections, Raymond Procunier, lockdowned[17] indefinitely all programs, work assignments, and recreational activities at San Quentin, Soledad, Folsom, and Deuel. California once again took the lead in penology: Procunier's termination of these programs in the most "Progressive" penal system in the country effectively marked the official reaction to rehabilitation and treatment in prison settings.

What caused the demise of rehabilitation and treatment programs? Was it related only to the radicalization of prisoners, to the riots, the strikes, and the insurrection at Attica, or were there other reasons for the end of the medical model? A group of relatively empirical and traditional criminologists set the stage for the end of rehabilitation in a number of academic studies written in the late 1960s and early 1970s. Most of these studies showed that rehabilitation and treatment made little if any difference in the recidivism rates of offenders. Although ideology fueled many of their works, their "hard" data convinced many of their colleagues in the correctional field. The strength of the data made it difficult for penologists to reject their argument. One influential book was Leslie Wilkins's *Evaluation of Penal Measures* (1969), based on a study of a variety of treatment programs that called into question the value of rehabilitative methods. Probably more important was Robert Martinson and his colleagues' study of treatment programs in New York, which resulted in the book *The Effectiveness of Correctional Treatment* (1975).[18] Along with prisoner activism, such academic studies effectively terminated the treatment model of penology.

Ironically, Governor Rockefeller himself brought together a Special Committee on Criminal Offenders to find effective ways to rehabilitate convicts late in 1971. The committee found that there was no information base for treatment methods of previous decades with which present treatment methods could be compared for their effectiveness—that is, no standards existed. Therefore, Martinson, Douglas Lipton, and Judith Wilks surveyed 231 studies that had been written between 1 January 1945 and 31 December 1967 and that had 285 separable findings. They asked two basic questions: What treatment methods were administered to criminal offenders? How effective were they in changing the offender or in reducing recidivism? Their findings were so disturbing that New York attempted to suppress their report. But Martinson persisted in publicizing the group's conclusions and published a summary in 1974 in the journal *Public Interest*,[19] and the full report came out in 1975.

In general, the report found that "with few and isolated exceptions, the rehabilitative efforts that have been reported so far have had no appreciable effect on recidivism." Martinson asked in his summary, "Do all these studies lead us irrevocably to the conclusion that nothing works, that we haven't the faintest clue about how to rehabilitate offenders and reduce recidivism? And if so, what shall we do?" To answer his own question, he attacked the whole notion of crime as a disease and stated the opposite position, that crime is a normal social phenomenon, an idea that leads away from treatment ideology.

For solutions, Martinson fell back on a variation of differential association.[20] He distinguished prisoners according to their potential for recidivism. He favored decarceration and community corrections for offenders at low risk of repeating their crimes, and imprisonment for hard-core transgressors with high potential for recidivism. This solution, however, leads to a new moral dilemma, because many low-recidivism-potential offenders are those who have committed serious crimes, such as murder. By Martinson's logic, if the person who murders will never murder again, such as the one who kills his or her adulterous spouse in a moment of passion, this offender would be decarcerated. But not placing a murderous offender in prison, Martinson also suggested, violates society's sense of justice and retribution. Therein lies a bind.

Martinson concluded by calling for an emphasis on deterrence at the expense of the treatment strategies that have so woefully failed. Perhaps, he speculated, stopping criminal behavior before it starts is the answer. In effect, he did not really know what would work, nor did he have an answer for the question of how to deter those who commit the passionate murder. The importance of his study, however, is that it supplies evidence that the treatment model had a brittle and unstable foundation and was ready to collapse.

At the same time that the radical criminologists and reformers were attacking the treatment model, another group came out against the prevailing system for a different reason and added moral force to the attack. The American Friends Service Committee (AFSC), a Quaker group active in the antiwar and civil rights movements, had members who had been incarcerated and who knew prison conditions firsthand. Earlier Quakers had been active in the invention of the penitentiary in the eighteenth century; these Quakers came out strongly against rehabilitation as it was practiced in the twentieth century. The AFSC published a report on crime and punishment, *Struggle for Justice,* in 1971. The report was based on a study of all criminal justice institutions, including the fortresslike prisons that dotted the American landscape.

The Quaker committee found that the whole criminal justice system was deeply imbued with class injustice: "The selection of candidates for prosecution reflects inequality in the larger society not only because of bias on the part of police or prosecutors but because the substantive content of the law affects those who are not social equals in quite different ways."[21] Not only does the system single out the lower (read: dangerous) classes for prosecution, the report continued, it supplies the judicial apparatus with the discretionary power to treat or change individuals' behavior in a way that protects those in control. The report singled out the treatment method as the main culprit in the failure of the prison system. By persuading offenders that they are sick, the treatment process destroys their character instead of building their pride and self-confidence. And in giving the discretionary power to treat to the same agencies responsible for protecting society, it indefinitely perpetuates the idea of the "sick" offender. In a very significant passage reminiscent of Kantian ethics, the report states: "We submit that the basic evils of imprisonment are that it denies autonomy, degrades dignity, impairs or destroys self-reliance, inculcates authoritarian values, minimizes the likelihood of beneficial interaction with one's peers, fractures family ties, destroys the family's economic stability, and prejudices the prisoner's future prospects for any improvement in his economic and social status."[22]

In conclusion, the Quakers called for changing the class-based criminal law; inflicting punishment on the basis of actual harm caused; shorter periods of humane incarceration; and offering help to those who seek it rather than imposing treatment and thereby depriving the prisoner of autonomy. This idea of the moral autonomy of the criminal, as advocated by radicals and Quaker theorists in the 1970s, eventually came full circle and converged with the reactionary "just deserts" view of punishment in the 1980s.

Inevitably, prisoners' activism and reformers' and academics' criticisms forced the federal government into making an official response. In 1971 the National Advisory Commission on Criminal Justice Standards and Goals met, and it issued its report on corrections in 1973. In true governmental fashion, it took the middle road through the theories and studies of the radicals, liberals, and reactionaries. The commission admitted that the system was too arbitrary and discretionary, but it was so only after a prisoner's conviction: "This high regard for the rule of law has been applied extensively in the criminal justice system up to the point of conviction. But beyond conviction, until recently, largely unsupervised and arbitrary discretion held sway. This was true of sentencing, for which criteria were absent and from which appeals were both rare and difficult. It was true of the discretion exercised by the institutional administrator concerning prison conditions and disciplinary sanctions."[23] The commission completely ignored the radicals' and Quakers' criticism that the

American criminal justice system was loaded against the lower classes, who bore the brunt of harsh punishment whether or not they were the most dangerous or committed the most crimes. That overhaul of the system was needed just as badly, if not more so, before the point of conviction as after.

In other reports the commission recognized that the American judicial system was inadequate and adversely affected the correctional system. But its solution dated back to the Era of Treatment and had been advocated by prisoner reformers for some years: community-based corrections. The experts on the commission thought that the extended use of this concept, giving prisoners the freedom to leave the institution to go to work or school, and turning away from the old fortresslike prisons would alleviate the abuses of the system.

The mega-institution, holding more than a thousand inmates, has been built in larger number and variety in this country than anywhere else in the world. Large institutions for young offenders have also proliferated here. In such surroundings, inmates become faceless people living out routine and meaningless lives. And where institutions are racially skewed and filled with a disproportionate number of ill-educated and vocationally inept persons, they magnify tensions already existing in our society. [24]

Although the commission recommended limiting discretionary decision-making and advocated additional prisoners' rights, taking action on these recommendations was politically infeasible. So the official penology in the 1970s once again became community corrections. Even some radical criminologists accepted the notion and incorporated it into their idea of popular justice.

Wherever possible, punishment is not alienated from the community. In the same way that there would be collective responsibility for an offense, there would be collective responsibility for punishment. . . . Such [community] surveillance would differ from "probation" or a "suspended sentence" in that members of the community would actively participate in the social control of the offender rather than having control handled by a probation bureaucracy. Similarly, if short-term incarceration facilities were necessary, they would be locally controlled and integrated into the general community. [25]

During the 1970s, halfway houses and community corrections centers proliferated throughout the United States. Some were limited to serving probationers, but most served parolees as well. Many problems, including the important problem of costs, beset these centers and caused their eventual failure.

Whether a prisoner was in a "community" institution or in a fortress, he was still incarcerated and not at liberty. Most convicts viewed these centers not as country clubs but as prisons; as a result, the rate of absconding was high. On the other hand, a large segment of the public *did* view the centers as country clubs and as not punitive enough to give them a sense of retribution. The high rate of escapes reinforced public antipathy to them and fed the flames of reactionaries who were increasingly emphasizing punishment at the expense of any form of treatment.

Moreover, few communities wanted the corrections centers located within their boundaries. Almost every time one was proposed, local residents vociferously protested. So most were set up in slums and ghettos—the very places whence the convicts had come. David Greenberg pointed out that instead of instilling bourgeois values through supportive community networks, just the opposite was happening—because penologists had no power to change the society or the community itself:

The National Advisory Commission's *Report on Corrections* . . . ignores the extent to which high levels of unemployment and structural features of the labor market may hinder the ex-offender from "pursuing a lawful style of living in the community." If it is true that lack of contact with good schools and adequate housing contributes to criminality and if there are no good schools or adequate housing in the community, how can a community corrections center remedy this? It is in no position to improve the schools or bring slum apartments into conformity with housing codes. [26]

Greenberg also pointed out that many convicts are already integrated into communities when they commit their offenses, but they are undesirable, criminal communities. And convicts might desire to return to them "in order to obtain financial rewards, status, and excitement."

Other complications led to the ultimate failure of community corrections. For one thing, halfway houses, educational and vocational training, and the like did not reduce prison expenses. They could be as expensive as incarceration; and in many instances community corrections cost more. Nor did the use (or misuse) of these programs reduce prison populations. The convicts likely to serve in community-based institutions were those who would not have been incarcerated under the old system either but would have been let off on probation or diverted in other ways. With the community corrections system, the criminal justice apparatus had an alternative to the traditional prison, and so these offenders were now sentenced to do time. Those who had committed more serious crimes were sent to prison anyway. The result was that throughout the 1970s the overall prison population soared to new heights. In 1970 there were 198,831 convicts in state and federal prisons; a decade later there were 302,377.[27] In addition, the number of convicts per 100,000 of population rose from 98 in 1970 to an all-time high of 133 in 1980.[28]

In sum, community corrections did not turn out to be a cure-all for rehabilitation but actually contributed to the backlash against rehabilitation and toward more punitive punishment. It did not reduce prison populations; it did not reduce prison expenses; and the public perception of "coddling" criminals that it created played into the hands of custody-minded officials who were advocating harsher punishment.

The 1970s began with prison activism and violence on a scale and of a quality hitherto unseen. It ended with the demise of the treatment model, the failure of the long-held concept of a community panacea for the ills of the carceral system, a breakdown in prisoners' unity, and a return to classical notions of punishment. The continuing failure of the prison system and the end of effective convict activism were even more glaring in the 1980s, which opened with one of the most violent prison riots in United States history: the uprising and slaughter at the New Mexico penitentiary at Santa Fe.

Chapter Seven

Reaction and Repression: The 1980s

Early on the morning of 2 February 1980, convicts took control of the New Mexico State Penitentiary at Santa Fe. By the following afternoon, thirty-three prisoners had been murdered, scores had been raped, beaten, and wounded, and eight hostage guards had been tortured. The Santa Fe riot was the bloodiest since Attica in 1971. But the similarity between the two uprisings ended there. Most significant, at Attica it had been law-enforcement officers who caused most of the carnage, whereas at Santa Fe prisoners killed prisoners.[1] The New Mexico riot—only one of many violent prison incidents during the 1980s—strikingly illustrates the changes both prisoners and keepers had undergone during the late 1970s and 1980s. The prison movement had turned on itself and devoured its political achievements.

Administrative and managerial conditions at Santa Fe had been deplorable. Barely three weeks before the riot, the state attorney general had completed an investigation that found, among other faults, poorly trained guards and woefully inadequate security measures. For their part, convicts had complained for years about overcrowding, bad food, and official brutality. They had filed a lawsuit charging that the prison was dangerously conducive to violence and rape. Contributing to this volatile situation, the small ill-trained staff used old-fashioned, petty disciplinary measures such as marching convicts single file in corridors and mandating short haircuts.

As in most riots, a minor incident sparked this one off: at 2 A.M. on Saturday, 2 February, four guards who were making night checks came upon a vat of home-brewed alcohol in a medium security dormitory.[2]

Under normal circumstances the liquor would have been confiscated, the incident would have been reported, and minor disciplinary action would have been taken. But the convicts, emboldened by a night of drinking the liquor, overpowered the guards. Within minutes the prisoners had grabbed the guards' keys, unlocked adjacent dormitories, and taken more hostages from among the guards. The riot quickly gathered momentum as the initiators pressured other convicts to participate, sometimes with force. A group of rioters stormed the control booth, and without much difficulty and to the great surprise of the guards within, they broke through the supposedly shatterproof window and sent its occupants running for safety. The fleeing guards left behind all the control keys, as well as tear-gas grenades, a launcher, and riot-control batons. Shortly thereafter, the convicts broke into the psychological unit, pillaged the files, broke up the furniture, and set the wreckage aflame. Then they opened up cell block 3, which held the most hardened and dangerous convicts. As one official said, "When they told me that people in cell block three were free, I said, there's death."[3]

He was correct in his prediction. The convicts roamed freely throughout the penitentiary opening up more units. At the plumbing shop they grabbed a heavy-duty acetylene torch and used it to cut through the grills of two other units, thereby releasing eighty-six more troops to take part in the imminent chaotic slaughter. Descending to the basement, they found that construction crews had left two torches behind. The convicts now had three acetylene torches and assorted other instruments of death.

Meanwhile, other rioters broke into the prison hospital, seized large quantities of drugs such as Demerol, Valium, phenobarbital, and methadone, and embarked on a mad frenzy of drug injections. Others broke into the paint and shoe shops and eagerly sniffed the paint thinner and glue stored there. Intoxicated from drugs, alcohol, and other substances, many went on a veritable orgy of vengeance and rage against the very physical plant of the institution. They destroyed everything in sight: tore out urinals, broke all the glass, smashed the furniture, and left behind a path of destruction throughout the prison.

Initially, the only violence against persons was against the hostages. Naked and bound, the hostages were beaten and stabbed by the convicts, who then sodomized them with riot sticks and ax handles and forced them to perform fellatio on their captors. Very soon, however, the convicts ferociously turned on themselves.

In most if not all prisons, management relies to some extent on a network of informers or "snitches" to maintain a degree of control. Convicts inform for a variety of reasons—revenge, hate, favors, fear. One former warden at Santa Fe remarked that whenever he saw two or more prisoners together, half of them belonged to him. Even though so many are involved in this game at one time or another, informers are the most hated breed in prison. When informers are identified, officials have to protect them from other inmates. Therefore, all prisons have what is called a protective custody unit to segregate not only snitches but also the weak, the victimized, the mentally ill, the despised child-molesters, defenseless homosexuals, and other outcasts of prison society. All activities in this unit—cell block 4 in Santa Fe—are carried out apart from other convicts. Those in protective custody eat and exercise together and remain totally isolated from the general prison population.

Shortly after the riot began, at around 3 A.M., the convicts' bloodthirst turned toward the snitches, both real and imagined. A group of rioters stopped in front of one cell and called the occupant an informer, despite his protests to the contrary. They opened the cell and savagely beat him with steel pipes. They left him barely alive—but only for a moment, as one member came back and finished him off with a pair of scissors. A different group of convicts stabbed another purported informer fifty times with a screwdriver and gouged his eyes out.

Other prisoners with larger and even more gruesome intentions used a torch to break through the grille of cell block 4, the protective custody wing. Between 4 A.M. and 7 A.M. the rioters methodically burned through the grille as the ninety-six prisoners inside screamed hysterically in anticipation of the tortures to come. At the same time, police and troopers were already surrounding the penitentiary, but they did nothing to save cell block 4. Later the officials explained that they didn't want to harm the hostages.

At 7 A.M. the convicts broke through 4–block's grille, and the massacre began. They mutilated, burned, beat to death, and threw both living and dead bodies from the tiers of the cell block. The brutality of the killing was horrendous, even to the most hardened convict: "Outside, a prison official hears a whistling sound from 4, scans the block with binoculars, stops on an incredible scene through a window, and watches in horror as four or five inmates hold a man down as another burns his head and face with a blowtorch. When his eyes explode out the back of his head, the inmates burn his groin, then mutilate the body with shanks, and torch him again."[4] The carnage and butchery in cell block 4 lasted less than an hour, but thirteen lives were lost by torch, pipe, sander, and other weapons. In one case the rioters couldn't open a cell, so they threw in flammable liquids and a match and watched the occupant burn to death. Even after the cell block 4 carnage ended, the blood ritual continued in the rest of the penitentiary. Six men from cell block F-1 were killed, and three from B-1. Some convicts set up a kangaroo court and meted out capital sentences. The brutality did not stop with death: "Several corpses [were] mutilated, then sodomized, the torsos left at grotesque angles."[5]

Only in the morning did negotiations between the rioters and the administration begin. The national guard had arrived by seven-thirty; at eight o'clock the convicts demanded to talk to reporters and Governor Bruce King or they would start killing the hostages. The governor arrived at the prison a little after nine o'clock and promised to meet with the convicts in the yard. (He did not keep his commitment.)

By the time the governor arrived, several nonrioting convicts had escaped from cell block 4 and had begun to relate the story of the massacre to officials; thus the administration was not ignorant of the gravity of the situation. At approximately the same time, the riot leaders—or what passed for leaders in this anarchic uprising—issued a list of demands that included a reduction in prison overcrowding, compliance with court orders, no retaliation against the rioters, and due process in classification procedures. These issues were mild in comparison to the prisoners' rights movement of the 1960s and 1970s; in fact, in 1976 New Mexico's attorney general and other state officials had signed a district court order that forced the penitentiary to improve those very classification procedures, reduce the overcrowding, improve the food and water supply, the plumbing, and the heating, and ameliorate other conditions. The New Mexico State Penitentiary had largely ignored this court order.

Not until 3 P.M. on Saturday did the deputy warden meet with three convict negotiators. He received another list of demands, most of which addressed specific grievances such as overcrowding, visiting conditions, and recreational and educational facilities.

Not until 8 A.M. on Sunday morning did three convict leaders sit down to begin serious negotiations with the warden, the deputy warden, the commissioner of corrections, a state senator, and a reporter. During these talks the officials signed an agreement that guaranteed that there would be no retaliation against the rioters. The no-retribution promise was reiterated by officials, and the convicts freed the hostages. The national guard, the state troopers, and a police SWAT team then assaulted the prison with violence almost as random as that of the riot itself. Although the troops retook the penitentiary within a brief period without firing a shot, they beat and humiliated the convicts, who put up little resistance.

The administration had regained control of a completely devastated institution. Thirty-three convicts were dead, and physically the prison was in ruins. Space for the convicts was quickly found: 90 went to Oklahoma, 148 to Leavenworth, 79 to Atlanta, and 30 to Colorado, among other places.

Shortly thereafter, the official investigations began and commissions issued reports. The New Mexico legislature authorized almost $90 million to repair the penitentiary, to build a new correctional institution, to conduct an investigation, and to prosecute the rioters (despite the no-retribution promise). The attorney general was authorized not only to investigate the causes of the riot but also to recommend changes in the administration of the penitentiary.

In June and September 1980 the attorney general's two-part inquiry into the riot appeared.[6] The report concluded that a series of security lapses had allowed convicts to gain control of the prison quickly. But the report stated that "these security lapses do not explain why the riot occurred in the first place."

The attorney general went on to blame a group of new, violent inmates who had gained leadership positions in the prison culture. His report did not blame the long history of brutality and corruption or the horrendous conditions in the prison. Although these conditions had existed for years, they had not hitherto precipitated such ferocious violence by themselves. To the extent that they were causative, however, removing them would logically have reduced motives for future violence. Following the riot, the administration made some improvements: it reduced the prison population by 40 percent, provided more training for officers, added recreational facilities, and instituted others changes. But within a year of the riot, nine convicts and two officers had been murdered in the penitentiary.

In May 1981 an independent report by attorney and consultant Daniel Cron came out. Cron detailed the penitentiary's severe and widespread violations of the law before the riot, including across-the-board disobedience of the standards mandated for maximum security inmates, inconsistent classification procedures, wholly unsatisfactory conditions for food preparation, unsafe and unsanitary living units, and an absence of reasonable provisions for the physical safety of the inmates. He also reported understaffing, unconstitutional tampering with inmates' mail, deficient medical care, poor access to legal help, dangerous wiring, defective plumbing, rat feces in food, and more.[7]

New Mexico stands out as the most brutal riot of the 1980s, but violence, uprisings, and disturbances continued at other prisons throughout the decade. Each year brought similar prison riots and other convict actions. At Pennsylvania's Graterford Prison a disturbance occurred in 1981 when a security-risk convict was given a low-security work assignment and proceeded to take three prisoners hostage. The same year there was another major riot at the Jackson, Michigan, penitentiary, the world's largest walled prison and the site of the 1952 riot. Sixty prisoners and seven guards were injured in a riot at San Quentin in 1982. For well over a year afterward, most of the three thousand prisoners were kept locked up, with little opportunity to move around freely. Despite this— or maybe because of the stress and pressure of being caged for such a long period—six deaths and sixty-six injuries occurred during the subsequent fifteen months. The warden called San Quentin a "monstrosity" and conceded he was "having trouble finding a solution to overcrowding, tension, food, sanitation and plumbing problems."[8]

At Attica in New York in 1983, 1700 convicts out of a total of 2,168 staged a work strike over what they considered the intolerable conditions in the institution. At the peak of the protest, this large percentage of the population refused to leave their cells for food, to participate in any programs, or to work in the shops. A group calling itself The Attica Inmate Population sent a letter stating, "We, the inmate population of the Attica Correctional Facility, are joining in a gesture of peaceful protest to the present conditions and policies of this facility . . . and want to demonstrate that we are common citizens and humans, and that is it only natural to protest for our civil and our human rights as the rest of us in the free society."[9] Two months later the Prisoners' Legal Services group of New York issued a report that confirmed the strikers' comments and stated that conditions had deteriorated to an "emergency situation." They had "been worsening steadily over the past few years. Racism, administrative indifference to grievances, physical brutality, the lack of meaningful programs for many inmates, no programs at all for many others, as well as an inadequate medical delivery system and other serious problems, simply degrade and dehumanize."[10]

In 1985 prisoners at New York's Sing Sing took several correctional officers hostage during a recreation period and began a siege that lasted two days. The same year, convicts at the maximum security section of the Indiana Reformatory at Pendleton took two employees hostage and wounded seven guards. Armed with homemade weapons, the prisoners were angry over what they considered abuse by the guards. They issued a list of twenty-two demands that included establishing a grievance committee, setting minimum wages for inmates, allowing prisoners to be politically active without intimidation or reprisals, and ending censorship of all letters, magazines, and newspapers.

At the Moundsville Penitentiary in West Virginia, convicts rose on New Year's Day 1986 and staged a bloody two-day riot during which three prisoners were killed. Later in the year, six convicts were killed and twelve injured. For want of a better explanation, one official (like the New Mexico attorney general in 1980) attributed the violence to younger inmates who appeared more willing to use violence to settle disputes.

That violence was endemic to the nation's prisons is hardly surprising, given the widespread brutal conditions. Courts were sentencing more people to prison (even as community corrections was becoming fashionable). In 1977 a major news magazine issued a special report called "Crisis in the Prisons: Not Enough Room for All the Criminals"[11] that highlighted prisons in Michigan, Maryland, Illinois, California, and North Carolina. At the Maryland State Penitentiary in Baltimore, for instance, an official stated, "If we emptied the prison today, we would be full tomorrow. . . . We are 100 percent overcrowded with another 100 percent waiting to get in." The second-oldest operating penitentiary in the country, Baltimore had at the time 1,530 prisoners, with an additional 1,080 in jails and other facilities.

Convicts in each prison system made the usual prison complaints of filth, poor medical care, and inadequate food. One prisoner said of the New Penology of the 1970s, "Prison life is deteriorating, and rehabilitation is a thing of the past. . . . There's no motivation and no incentive."[12] Stateville prison in Joliet, Illinois, which had been under strict control during the Joseph Ragen era, was apparently slipping back into the old chaos and violence. Over ten thousand prisoners shared cells that were equipped for four thousand; complaints again included poor food, inadequate medical attention, and the volatile, violent atmosphere. At Central Prison in Raleigh, North Carolina, 1,698 convicts occupied space designed for 800.

These examples are not extraordinary. In almost every state in the nation, prisons were operating either at or over capacity. In 1983 systems in at least forty states held over the maximum number of prisoners, and more than thirty states were operating under court orders because of lack of sufficient space. Almost every state was in the midst of some prison construction. At the same time, statistics show, there was a rise in the number of convicts on probation and parole. In 1983, for example, the parole population increased by 12.1 percent to a record high of 251,708, while the probation population reached a high of 1,502,247. Clearly more people were not only being convicted and sentenced to prison but were being released early. Yet the carceral network was still vastly overcrowded and getting worse.

The continuing sad state of the carceral system is partially a result of the prison activism of the two previous decades, which only resulted in crowding the prisons more. As mentioned in chapter 6, the ideas of prisoners' rights activists and reactionary conservatives converged and produced a new mentality among both groups. Their strange alliance brought about the demise of the rehabilitation model and ushered in the current period of "just deserts"—a reversion to neo-Kantian notions of punishment. Both reactionary lawmakers and politically radical convicts asserted the moral autonomy of the convicted offender who should get his just deserts according to the gravity of the offense—a neo-Kantian demand for retribution against a social enemy coupled with a utilitarian measure of punishment.

Like many "reforms" in the twentieth century, this movement started in California, where the 1960s and 1970s had brought the whole prison system, controlled by the Adult Authority, under attack. In 1976 the California Indeterminate Sentence Act had been in effect for almost sixty years. According to one source, this law stayed in place for so long because it released some officials from responsibility while serving as a useful control measure for others.

For years this system was satisfactory to a wide spectrum of opinion, and even when it came under heavy attack it seemed likely to endure because of the difficulty of agreeing on a replacement. The indeterminate sentence appeased liberal sensitivities by purporting to reject such "primitive" notions as retribution and deterrence, and by providing the possibility of speedy release of offenders amenable to rehabilitation. Judges were happy to be relieved of much responsibility and pressure inherent in sentencing. Prison administrators considered a flexible date of release an important tool in controlling hostile inmate populations. Politicians were free to be irresponsible: statutory penalties could be raised to grossly unrealistic levels to appease public passions without necessarily affecting the exercise of Adult Authority discretion. Law enforcement officials took comfort because it was possible to confine a "dangerous" prisoner for a very long time even if he could not be proved guilty in court of an exceptionally serious crime, and because many Adult Authority members came from law enforcement backgrounds. . . . One of the most useful features of delegating sentencing authority to the Adult Authority was that it made it possible for the legislature to avoid making hard decisions about how severely crime should or could be punished.[13]

Prisoners' rights groups had rightly seen that the concept of rehabilitation meant that two prisoners who had committed the same crime would be treated in different ways, depending on how they behaved in prison. One might serve three years for the same type of robbery for which another served one; the difference resulted from playing the prison behavior game. The arbitrariness was a source of extreme frustration: "Although there's no way to gather data on this that I know of, I am personally convinced, at any rate, that most of the violence in [California] prisons is caused . . . by the frustration and the bitterness and the rage and the despair which results from [a prisoner] not knowing how long he has to be there and from a certain group of people having *complete* control over the decision, the capriciousness and arbitrariness of that system."[14]

From the other end of the political spectrum, conservatives thought that the Adult Authority released convicts too quickly. They believed that punishment, isolation, and deterrence were the prime reasons for imprisonment in the first place, and they wanted to keep convicts off the street and know exactly how long they would be locked up. They did not want an arbitrary body such as the Adult Authority, which might be dominated by "prisoners' rights liberals," to have complete discretion over release. And the public demanded that someone take responsibility for what was perceived as rampant lawlessness, criminal-coddling, and early release under indeterminate sentence.

Therefore, to conservatives and liberals alike, determinate sentencing seemed a reform whose time has come.[15] The wheel turned full circle as a procedure that had failed in the past was perceived as a reform.

Thus in 1974, lawmakers introduced into the California legislature a bill to change the sentencing process. In September 1976, after several amendments and permutations, Governor Edmund G. Brown signed the bill into law (it became operative on 1 July 1977), approximately sixty years after the Indeterminate Sentence Act was passed. The treatment model, which one conservative colloquially termed "pap for the feint [*sic*] hearted,"[16] was legislated out of existence. The new law stated that the "purpose of imprisonment for crime is punishment."

Besides reconceiving the role of the prison in the criminal justice system, the new law had specific concrete meanings for convicts.[17] For one, "capital cases," or those sentences that are alternatives to the death penalty, retained the indeterminateness of seven years to life; the convict had to serve seven years before being eligible for parole. The law eliminated minimum and maximum sentences for approximately three hundred felonies for which commitment to prison was possible but not necessary. (It did not, however, have a significant effect on the judge's ability to grant probation in such cases.) These felonies were classified into four categories according to severity. Some of the crimes in each category included: 1) Murder in the second degree, rape with force or violence, exploding a destructive device causing bodily harm. 2) Robbery in the first degree by a person armed with a firearm, safecracking, kidnapping, burglary in the first degree. 3) Robbery in the second degree, arson, assault with deadly weapon, bribery of a public officer. 4) Grand theft, burglary in the second degree, forgery, car theft. In all, there were 181 other-than-capital offenses distributed in the four categories as follows: 1) 3; 2) 15; 3) 42; 4) 121. The judge could reduce many of the crimes to misdemeanors.

Within each category a choice of three penalties was offered:

1. 5 years, 6 years, 7 years
2. 3 years, 4 years, 5 years
3. 2 years, 3 years, 4 years
4. 16 months, 2 years, 3 years

The law directed the judge to select the middle penalty for most of the offenders. He could pick the lower penalty for mitigating circumstances and the higher for hardened or repeat offenders.

In place of the various incentives (such as the vague rehabilitation therapy) for early release available under the indeterminate sentence, the new law reverted to the older practice of "good time" credits. All prisoners except lifers could get up to one-third off their sentences for good behavior. For every twelve months the convict served, he could win three months for good behavior and one month for participation in work, educational, vocational, therapeutic, or other prison programs. Thus, a prisoner with a six-year sentence could be released in four years. (It was also more difficult to take away good time because of a vesting provision for credits earned each year.) After a convict's release, the law required one year of supervision regardless of time served in prison—again, except for lifers, who were supervised for three years after parole.

Other states quickly followed California's lead. In 1976 Maine abolished parole but left the fixing of maximum terms to the discretion of the judge. Indiana passed a new sentencing law in the same year, while Pennsylvania, Arkansas, Ohio, Hawaii, Colorado, and Delaware enacted statutes lengthening prison sentences but not necessarily changing the sentencing structure.[18]

Throughout the 1980s, the call for changes in sentencing laws swept the country. The federal government became caught up in the tide, and the Reagan administration created the United States Sentencing Commission as a result of the 1984 Comprehensive Crime Control Act (which had been passed in the Senate by a vote of 91 to 1 and 316 to 91 in the House). In September 1986 the commission published draft guidelines that specifically stated that the rehabilitation of a criminal was of secondary importance to protecting the public and that sentences should reflect the seriousness of the crime committed. The commission issued the final set of guidelines, which were to take effect on 1 November 1987. A proposal in the House of Representatives to delay their implementation for nine months was defeated by a vote of 231 to 183. Therefore, at the end of 1987 the federal government officially killed the rehabilitation ideal. To finalize the matter, on 19 January 1989 the U.S. Supreme Court upheld the constitutionality of the Sentencing Commission in an eight-to-one decision.

The commission mandated that every federal crime fell into one of forty-three different categories, under a complicated point system.[19] Higher categories reflected more serious crimes, and these offenders received more severe sentences. The computation of sentencing works as follows. Let us take the example of a burglar who has been convicted of stealing $15,000 from a residence, using a firearm. The base Offense Level for burglary is 17. Since the burglary involved a firearm, two more levels are added, bringing the Offense Level to 19. The judge can also levy more time according to the monetary amount the burglar stole. For amounts between $10,001 and $50,000, the judge can add two more levels, and he does so. This brings our burglar to Offense Level 21.

To determine the sentence, one turns to the sentencing table, on which the Offense Level forms the vertical axis (1 to 43) and the Criminal

History Category forms the horizontal axis (I to V). For the Criminal History Category, if a convict has served a prior sentence, he receives additional time. Our burglar previously served a sentence exceeding one year and one month; he therefore receives three points, putting him in Criminal History Category II. The intersection of Offense Level 21 on the vertical axis and Criminal History Category II on the horizontal axis gives a sentence of from forty-one to fifty-one months.

A repeat offender can end up with a sentence higher than the statutory limits. In such cases, the commission treats the offender as a lifer.

Judges have the discretion to sentence within the range provided. If he sentences outside the range, he has to cite in writing the aggravating or mitigating factors. The commission abolished the parole system: Convicts have to serve their full sentence. But as in California, they can earn good time credits. (However, the commission sharply curtailed good time provisions in existence under previous statutes.)

The implementation of these determinate sentencing laws effectively cut off the treatment model from the criminal sanction. As in conservative penologist Norval Morris's 1970s call for a "noncoercive prison," facilitated change replaced coercive cure, and graduated testing for fitness for freedom replaced parole prediction of suitability for release.[20] In this noncoercive type of prison, "prisoners are freed from the discretionary authority of their prison and parole administrators that formerly tied their freedom to program participation. Opportunities for self-improvement would be offered but participation would no longer be made a condition of release. While treatment is not to be coerced, change would be facilitated."[21]

In other words, in the new system punishment is to be fair and equitable, but the only purpose of imprisonment is punishment. This principle is clear, for example, in the 1987 "Action Agenda Plan for Maryland State Prisons" issued by the state's Joint Legislative/Executive Committee on Corrections Capital Planning. In this plan the emphasis is primarily on housing and classifying convicts for security risk rather than on rehabilitation programs. In fact, the buzzword used in this and similar reports is now *reintegration* rather than *rehabilitation*.

During the 1980s the community corrections model of the 1960s and 1970s has joined with the classical model of "just deserts." The new sentencing procedures did not abolish work release, halfway houses, nonresidential community corrections centers, educational furloughs, or other decarceration programs, but they were added to the mixture.

The hardening of attitudes toward crime and punishment had specific effects on the nation's corrections system. A 1977 Rand Corporation report projected that although determinate sentencing could reduce crime by 20 percent under certain conditions, the prison population would increase by 85 percent; a crime reduction of 30 percent would triple the prison population.[22] By the late 1980s, the determinate sentence and the law-and-order attitude of the public and conservative governments had in fact brought about a tremendous crisis of overcrowding in prisons, and consequently the nation's penal system is in almost total disarray.

Statistics reveal the proportions of this crisis. In 1970 prisons held 328,000 offenders. In April 1988 there were 581,609 convicts, an increase of 6.7 percent from twelve months before. In September 1988 a record 604,824 prisoners resided in state and federal prisons—up 4 percent in the first six months of the year. Between 1970 and 1988, the prison population increased by 85 percent.

The increase in number of convicts per 100,000 population is even more significant. In 1970 it was 96, in 1980 it was 138, and at the end of 1987 it was 228—a 137 percent increase since 1970. This figure does not even take into account the inevitable increase in convicts currently resulting from the federal Determinate Sentencing Act. A National Council on Crime and Delinquency study released in April 1988 projected that there would be an additional 20 percent increase in the prison population by 1992. The number of federal prisoners alone is expected to rise to 165,000 in the year 2002, from its present 48,300.

The vanguard state of California has seen its prison population explode from 24,569 at the end of 1980 to 68,139 in April 1988. More convicted felons were ending up in prison rather than on probation or in other decarceral alternatives, and sentences were longer—much to the chagrin of prisoners and others who had previously and rightly blamed long terms on the indeterminate sentence. In Illinois, for example, the percentage of felony sentences that included imprisonment rose from 36 percent in 1975 to 42 percent in 1985. And even before the Determinate Sentencing Act went into effect, the average lengths of prison sentences given out in federal courts increased by 32 percent between 1979 and 1986, reflecting the harsher law-and-order mentality of both the public and the government.

The officials and lawmakers in charge had not taken into account in their new laws (except in a few states, such as Minnesota[23]) that most jurisdictions did not have the capacity to handle so many new prisoners. And if convicts now agreed that they had moral autonomy in committing and paying for their crimes, they expected at the very least decent conditions of imprisonment. When they did not get them but instead were packed like sardines into cans, they went to the courts, and they often won.

Just as more and more jurisdictions were "getting tough" on crime and passing stricter sentencing laws, the convicts were suing over what they and many prisoners' rights lawyers considered the "cruel and unusual punishment" of prison conditions. The convicts asserted that overcrowding led to

1. continual and abnormal violence, including sexual assaults;
2. poor health and the spread of diseases among inmates;
3. the increasing idleness and stagnation of prison life, as recreational, vocational, and educational programs have to be cut back;
4. total loss of privacy and inhuman suffering as more and more inmates are forced to share cells designed for the occupancy of fewer people or dormitories in which almost every inch of available space is occupied by a bunk or mattress. [24]

The late 1970s and early 1980s saw a spate of court cases against such conditions in the nation's penal system. A far-reaching decision that affected one of the largest correctional systems in the country was Texas's *Ruiz v. Estelle* case.

David Ruiz, a Texas prisoner who had often been segregated from the general prison population because of his violence against other convicts, charged in court that the conditions in solitary confinement in which he lived were inhumane. In 1974 the court placed Ruiz's petition along with seven others under a class action suit. The Ruiz case came to trial in 1978 and lasted 159 days. On 12 December 1980 the judge handed down a decision that ordered sweeping changes in the Texas system.

Among other issues, the judge's ruling found the whole Texas correctional system abusive and restrictive, its prisons overcrowded, and its classification system inadequate. Although litigation lingered on for a few more years and a court of appeals overturned several provisions of the ruling, the system itself was declared unconstitutional. The case was finally settled in 1985. [25]

The Ruiz case was only the most outstanding example in a broad trend toward judicial intervention into the nation's carceral system. It was also a logical outgrowth of the movement toward—in fact, back to—courts defining prison terms to a greater extent than the professional corrections people of the Era of Treatment. By 1987, approximately forty state prison systems and many of the largest city and county jails were operating under court orders because of overcrowding and/or poor conditions. A recent study on overcrowding in prisons concluded:

Overcrowded prisons have higher rates of inmate-inmate violence and higher levels of various indicators of inmate mental and physical disease. Research to date has not determined the magnitude of the independent causal effect of overcrowding on those measures of prison conditions and effects. It appears that overcrowding, in interaction with age and housing arrangements, accounts for substantial amounts of explained variation in levels of inmate violence and health. . . . Increased idleness, inappropriate housing assignments, overclassification, insufficient program resources, decreased staff training, and increased stress on staff result from overcrowding. While research on these consequences of overcrowding is lacking, experience suggests that such outcomes are routinely observable.[26]

The system is thus locked in a bind. Overcrowding will continue as long as sentencing laws are strict and more convicts spend time in prison. At the end of the 1980s, a change toward leniency does not seem likely. Politicians ultimately control the system, and they will always reflect the public's attitude toward crime. And that attitude now says to lock up criminals. To the majority of the public, cells alone are meaningful for criminals. So caged the convict must be.

The first response to this dilemma—to build more prison cells—did not take into account counterarguments such as

1. The United States already imprisons a greater proportion of its population than nearly any other country.
2. The costs of building are huge.
3. The arguments typically advanced for building that rest on deterrence and incapacitation are not supported by the scientific evidence.
4. There are sound ethical reasons to seek a reduction in the use of imprisonment.[27]

Nevertheless, states across the nation have gone on a building frenzy, spending $4 billion on new prison construction since 1981. Construction costs for prisons range from $50,000 to $75,000 per cell.[28] These figures do not take into account that it costs $12,000 to $30,000 a year to maintain a typical prisoner in an institution. More new prisons and prisoners also mean, of course, that additional personnel are needed to guard and train the convicts. The upsurge in confinements in New York City, for example, led to a 173 percent increase in Department of Corrections personnel over one decade. (At the end of fiscal year 1978 the department had 4,061 employees; on 30 June 1988 it had 7,016.) Over the same period the number of full-time city employees increased by only 17.4 percent.[29]

This trend is taking place all over the United States. Statistics show that the number of convicts increases and outpaces capacity no matter how much building goes on. In April 1988, Allen F. Breed of the National Council on Crime and Delinquency remarked, "Nationwide we're still putting about 750 more inmates in prison each week than we're releasing." With more and more violent drug-related crime occurring in the cities, it does not seem that the number of prisoners will soon abate or that the public's attitude will soften. The only real possibility of a downturn is in the demographics of the country. The reduction in the number of men in the most crime-prone age group—from the teens to mid-twenties—that seems likely because of the lower birth rate over the last two decades could bring a downturn in crime and conviction rates. But such a reduction is only hypothetical, for less numerous teens could also turn out to be more violent and commit more crimes.

Although the public wants more prisons, voters do not necessarily like to pay their skyrocketing costs. For instance, in New York the electorate recently defeated a bond issue to increase prison capacity. This contradictory attitude (along with the spread of the deadly AIDS virus in prisons) is forcing professionals in and out of government to devise new alternatives to incarceration for nonviolent offenders and to offer more options between probation and imprisonment. Some of the new alternatives include more intensive probation-supervision programs, electronic monitoring of decarcerated offenders, drug therapy, and the privatization of corrections.

As jurisdictions release more and more minor offenders, effective probation-supervision methods are increasingly needed. By the late 1980s, approximately forty-five jurisdictions had implemented intensive probation-supervision programs as alternatives to incarceration. These programs generally include restitution and work assignments, curfews, and blood and urine testing for controlled substances and alcohol. Another program is split sentencing, which combines probation with confinement in community corrections programs or with brief periods of regular imprisonment so the convict does not get off "easy."[30] However, a congressional report has raised the question that these programs may discriminate, violating the Constitution's equal protection and due process clauses, if the candidates are categorized or classified in ways that the Supreme Court finds suspect.[31]

Another alternative to incarceration is the electronic monitoring of decarcerated offenders. In the mid-1980s, courts started to opt for high-technology monitoring of probationers and parolees rather than for keeping them confined.

As long ago as 1964, Harvard professor Ralph Schwitzgebel had envisioned a system of electronic parole to monitor parolees' behavior twenty-four hours a day. Tracking devices were tested in Cambridge and Boston between 1964 and 1970. In 1977, Judge Jack Love of New Mexico reportedly came up with the idea independently after reading a *Spiderman* cartoon magazine in which a villain attaches an electronic bracelet to the hero's wrist to keep track of him. Love convinced one Michael Goss, a computer salesman, to develop such an instrument. Goss established National Incarceration Monitor and Control Services and began marketing the devices.[32] In 1985, Michigan put the devices into use. By 1987, forty-five corrections agencies were using them to track parolees, defendants under house arrest, and those on probation.

The system usually consists of three components:

1. a transmitter device worn by the offender around the ankle, neck, or wrist, which transmits an encoded signal at regular intervals over a range of approximately 200 feet;

2. a receiver unit located in the offender's home that detects signals from the transmitter and periodically reports to a central computer;

3. a control computer located at the criminal justice center that accepts reports from the receiver unit over telephone lines, compares them with the offender's curfew schedule, and alerts correctional personnel to unauthorized absences.[33]

The idea, of course, is to remind the convict that he is under constant, round-the-clock surveillance. Such a surveillance system widens the range of social control and is used for low-risk offenders; the most serious and repeat convicted felons are not put into this system. In effect, electronic surveillance is an attempt to monitor and control the convict's total life, a system almost analogous to Jeremy Bentham's eighteenth-century concept of the Panopticon prison, in which convicts are placed under surveillance around the clock from a central control station. It is

132 *The Prison Reform Movement*

easy to see that civil libertarians will raise constitutional questions about the use of such repressive devices. So far, however, no court cases or opinions have resulted, and many convicts have opted for this alternative as less intrusive than going to prison.

Another alternative to imprisonment that has appeared recently is drug therapy, especially for those who have committed sex offenses or crimes related to alcohol abuse. The drug Antabuse, which when combined with alcohol makes the person violently ill, is used in lieu of imprisonment for drunk drivers, chronic disorderly conduct offenders, and the like. The technique of chemical castration is also practiced upon some sex offenders. Antiandrogenprogesterone drugs such as Depo-Provera manipulate the hormones to decrease a person's sexual drive and activity. First used in the 1960s in West Germany and Switzerland, the U.S. Food and Drug Administration has not yet approved it for general treatment of sexual deviants.

Even though these probationary methods have increasingly been used in the 1980s, a 1985 Rand Corporation study reported that of its sample population of probationers from Los Angeles and Alameda counties, 65 percent were arrested again, 51 percent were convicted of new crimes, and 34 percent were placed on probation again. Not surprisingly, the repeaters usually committed burglary, theft, and robbery. The study also found little evidence that imprisonment itself diminishes the likelihood of recidivism. And: "Judging by our statistical model of who would succeed on probation, only three percent of the felons sentenced to California prisons qualified as good probation risks."[34] The results of the new, intensive surveillance are not in yet, but the number of convicts presently involved in the programs is so small that it is unlikely that anything definitive will come out of current studies.

As neither probation nor imprisonment reduced crime and recidivism rates and as the Reagan era brought in a conservative tendency to privatize certain governmental functions, corrections officials also turned to private industry to alleviate their problems. In March 1988 the President's Commission on Privatization issued the report *Privatization: Toward More Effective Government,*[35] which recommended, among other things, that

1. contracting should be regarded as an effective and appropriate form for the administration of prisons and jails at the federal, state, and local levels;

2. proposals to contract for the administration of entire facilities at the federal, state, or local level ought to be seriously considered;

3. problems of liability and accountability should not be seen as posing insurmountable obstacles to contracting for the operation of confinement facilities. Constitutional and legal requirements apply, and contracted facilities may also be required to meet American Correctional Association standards.[36]

Privatization is nothing new; it is a variation on the old contract and leasing system that was prevalent in the nineteenth and early twentieth centuries. By 1987, more than three dozen states had contracted out at least one and sometimes more services to private firms. The most commonly contracted services involved mental and medical health, education, vocational training, drug treatment, counseling, and construction. Some jurisdictions, however, have contracted out entire prisons. In 1986, for example, The U.S. Corrections Corporation opened a private, three-hundred-bed state prison in Kentucky for convicts who are within three years of coming before the parole board. That Kentucky is the state with the first entirely private prison is significant because the idea of contracting prisons began there in 1825, when Joel Scott leased the state's entire prison population for use in industry. In 1985 the Corrections Corporation of America failed to take over the entire prison system of Tennessee; but back in 1894 that state had leased its convict population to the Tennessee Coal and Iron Railroad for a yearly payment of $100,000.

Much controversy surrounds the private sector's involvement in the prison business. Certainly, private corporations are primarily concerned with maximizing profits and do not operate for long at a loss. And the nation's earlier experience with the leasing and contract system shows that the profit-maximization occurs at the expense of the convict's welfare. Effective government regulation of private business has not been a priority in the conservative climate of the 1980s. A more important and fundamental consideration, however, is that government is relinquishing its responsibility to care for its social enemies, convicted offenders. A philosophical question arises: Can government delegate to a private business its authority to coerce, deprive liberty, punish, and even kill?

Some of these issues have been raised in the courts and address the constitutional question "whether the acts of a private entity operating a correctional institution constitute 'state action,' and whether delegation of the corrections function to a private entity is itself constitutional."[37] A number of state and federal courts have already ruled in favor of private entities performing acts delegated them by the state.[38] The concept of delegation itself is less clear cut, however. In the 1985 U.S. Court of Appeals case *Ancata v. Prison Health Services,* it was found that

> there is an area of overlap between state action and the propriety of a delegation of governmental powers: Government liability cannot be reduced or eliminated by delegating the governmental function to a private entity. But the nondelegation doctrine goes further than that, holding that some governmental functions may not be delegated *at all.* Whether the privatization of corrections would be held invalid under that doctrine is debatable; certainly the answer to that question is less clear than is the answer to the question whether such a delegation constitutes state action.[39]

Clearly, the courts will eventually have to confront these issues because the trend is toward privatization in the Reagan and Bush administrations.[40] By the end of the 1980s, only a small percentage of convicts are still affected by private business; from 1977 to 1987 only .2 percent of the prison population came into contact with private contracting. Compared with the large number of adult males in America who are under correctional supervision (about 3 percent in 1986), the number affected seems small. However, the trend is there. Privatization has not worked in the past and raises grave moral and philosophical questions that have little hope of successful resolution.

Another alternative to traditional imprisonment that has generated some controversy is the prison furlough. Used in nearly every prison system in the country, the program usually grants convicts furloughs near the end of their prison sentence to assist their transition into free society. Many furlough programs are also designed to alleviate overcrowding and range from four hours in Florida to 210 days in Oregon. Thirty-six state systems, the District of Columbia system, and the federal system allow murderers who are eligible for parole to apply for furloughs also. In 1987 most states reported success with the programs, meaning that the convicts committed no crimes (or were not caught committing crimes) while on furlough. For instance, Mississippi, Nevada, North Dakota, South Dakota, Wisconsin, and Washington all reported 100 percent success rates in their programs, while most other states reported success rates of over 90 percent. Whether these statistics are significant is another matter. Basically, the furlough is supposed to be a form of early parole for low-risk convicts who will soon be out of prison.

It is only the sensational case that catches public attention. For instance, the Massachusetts furlough program became a leading issue in the 1988 presidential campaign when the Republicans publicized the case of a Massachusetts convict who committed rape while on furlough. The thousands of other convicts on furlough who do not commit crimes were rarely mentioned.

As prisoners serve longer sentences, the problem of how to care for older prisoners has also affected the penal system. Most prisons are geared to convicts who range in age from their mid-teens to their thirties, not to those forty and above. The American Correctional Association found in a June 1988 study of forty-three state prison systems that there were 18,801 prisoners over the age of fifty-five—a 50 percent increase since 1984. The aging of the prison population raises such questions as special diets, housing, and medical care for chronic illnesses. One study found that the elderly convict suffers from an average of three chronic illnesses, tripling the cost of his care from a yearly average of $23,000 to over $70,000.

Compounding the problems created by overcrowding and other prison conditions, in the 1980s the convict population was struck heavily by the deadly AIDS virus. In 1988, AIDS was the single most important cause of death in prison populations. In New York, for instance, AIDS has been responsible for more than 50 percent of all convict fatalities since 1984. Another New York State study found that 15 percent of convicts entering the system were infected with the AIDS virus. The New York City health commissioner estimated that half of the 100,000 people who passed through the city's prison system were current or former intravenous drug users and that half of these were probably infected with the AIDS virus. The implications of these statistics are staggering. Most criminal justice officials are opposed to segregating prisoners carrying the virus unless they need medical treatment, and therefore the infection and mortality rates are increasing. The projected expense of this treatment is overwhelming.

AIDS is one more major complication that penologists and prison officials will have to face in the coming years. The fact that the carceral system has failed so badly during the last two centuries does not give us reason for optimism that any of these problems will be solved. Is there any hope for the future?

As we enter the 1990s the future of imprisonment appears bleaker than ever. We have gone from retribution to rehabilitation and back to retribution. The liberal stance has failed. Both liberals and conservatives now agree that something must be done with state-defined enemies of society and that previous penal practices have not succeeded in ameliorating behavior to any great extent. What is to be done with criminals? Only the most utopian penologists call for the total abandonment of prisons. Many radical criminologists and penologists rightly link the success or failure of prisons with structural transformations of society, but unfortunately, their solutions depend on radical social change, whose prospects seem hopelessly dim. In the meantime, technocrats—with the approbation of conservatives—are devising better and more efficient ways to control social deviants, whether in or out of prison. We are seeing only the beginning of the use of new technologies for total surveillance and punishment.

Penology has shifted to harsher punishments and tighter methods of social control. All punitive institutions are part of a larger network that permeates all of society, a "carceral network," as Michel Foucault correctly called it. This network in turn is affected by the larger social climate. The social climate of the late 1980s and early 1990s calls for strict conformity to certain conservative moral values. Antiabortion forces, school prayer advocates, religious fundamentalists, reactionary and neoconservative educational reformers, and the like have all gained power during the last decade and have pressured politicians and governmental bureaucrats into more conservative positions on these and other issues. As these advocates seek to recriminalize actions such as abortion and bring practitioners back into the deviant and carceral fold, the concept of crime itself is thus being redefined. In the same spirit, the death penalty is now being used and carried out frequently, and noncapital criminals receive heavier and longer sentences. The dominant trend is certainly toward a stricter punitive control apparatus that heavily emphasizes incarceration or technological surveillance over the more traditional Progressive methods of fines, probation, and parole.

Convicts themselves, as I have tried to show, agree with the neoclassical focus on the criminal act itself and the convict's concomitant moral autonomy in committing and paying for the action. Therefore, conservatives and convicts agree on the necessity of the criminal suffering pain as a consequence of his evil action. But how much pain? On this question the prisoners rejoin the liberals. Despite their loss of faith in treatment and rehabilitation, liberal reformers now emphasize care and humane conditions in the handling of convicts. The American Correctional Association's 1986 *Public Policy for Correction—a Manual for Decision-Mak-*

ers calls for more humane prisons. If one is going to endure punishment, pain, and suffering, such liberal documents ask, let it be done with standards that emphasize humanity, dignity, and moral autonomy.

If we have learned anything from the history of prison reform, it is that someday the rehabilitation ideal will return in some form, just as the current "just deserts" model is a throwback to retribution theories of the past. They will in all likelihood be a failure today, just as they were before.

Prisons exist in society, and as long as society does not undergo a deep and radical structural transformation, there is little chance that institutions, especially coercive ones, will be qualitatively changed. Perhaps then the best we can hope for, as long as we have prisons, is a measure of humanity in the way we treat criminals, outcasts, and deviants.

Notes and References

Chapter One

1. Motto of the New York Prison Association, founded in 1844.
2. On the relationship between sin, evil, and temporal punishment, the writings of Augustine have been extremely influential in the intellectual history of the West. See Herbert A. Deane, *The Political and Social Ideas of St. Augustine* (New York: Columbia University Press, 1963).
3. For an anthropological and religious explication of this view, see the important work by René Girard, *Violence and the Sacred* (Baltimore: Johns Hopkins University Press, 1977). Also see Friedrich Nietzsche, *The Genealogy of Morals* (New York: Doubleday, 1956).
4. The legal concept of confinement rather than punishment was formulated in the Justinian Code (A.D. sixth century), which stated, "*Carcer enim ad continendos homines non ad puniendos haberi debet*" ("Prisons exist only in order to keep men, not to punish them"), *Digest,* 48.19.8. The Romans frequently enslaved conquered foreigners. The Germanic tribes in the early Middle Ages had a system of fines, called wergild, that were imposed for a variety of crimes, including murder.
5. John Howard, *The State of the Prisons in England and Wales,* 4th ed. (1792; reprint, Montclair, N.J.: Patterson Smith, 1973). On utilitarianism and punishment, see works of Jeremy Bentham (1748–1832) such as *The Rationale of Punishment* (1830) and *Panopticon or Inspection House* (1791). In the latter, Bentham proposed a circular or polygonal architectural model of a prison in which prisoners would be visible at all times from a central guard station.
6. Quoted in James Heath, *Eighteenth Century Penal Theory* (London: Oxford University Press, 1963), 272.
7. Hugo A. Bedau, "Retribution and the Theory of Punishment," *Journal of Philosophy* 75 (1978): 601–20; Ted Honderich, *Punishment: Its Supposed Justification* (Baltimore: Penguin Books, 1971); Francis A. Allen, *The Decline of the Rehabilitative Ideal: Penal Policy and Social Purpose* (New Haven, Conn.: Yale

139

University Press, 1981); A. Von Hirsch, *Doing Justice* (New York: Hill and Wang, 1976); E. Van Den Haag, *Punishing Criminals* (New York: Basic Books, 1975).

8. For literature on reform in the early nineteenth century, see, among others, Edward Pessen, *Jacksonian America: Society, Personality, and Politics* (Homewood, Il.: The Dorsey Press, 1969); Clifford E. Griffin, *Their Brothers' Keepers: Moral Stewardship in the United States, 1800–1865* (New Brunswick, N.J.: Rutgers University Press, 1960); Charles C. Cole, *The Social Ideas of the Northern Evangelists, 1826–1860* (New York: Columbia University Press, 1954); Ronald G. Walters, *American Reformers, 1815–1860* (New York: Hill and Wang, 1978); Raymond A. Mohl, *Poverty in New York, 1783–1825* (New York: Oxford University Press, 1971); Carl F. Kaestle, *Pillars of the Republic: Common Schools and American Society, 1780–1860* (New York: Hill and Wang, 1983); Carroll Smith Rosenberg, *Religion and the Rise of the American City: The New York City Mission Movement, 1812–1870* (Ithaca, N.Y.: Cornell University Press, 1971); and especially David J. Rothman, *The Discovery of the Asylum: Social Order and Disorder in the New Republic* (Boston: Little, Brown, 1971).

9. Larry E. Sullivan, "Books, Power, and the Development of Libraries in the New Republic: The Prison and Other Journals of John Pintard of New York," *Journal of Library History* 21 (Spring 1986): 407–24.

10. Arthur A. Ekirch, Jr., "Thomas Eddy and the Beginnings of Prison Reform in New York," *New York History* 24 (July 1943): 376–91; Samuel Knapp, *Life of Thomas Eddy* (New York: Connor and Cooke, 1834).

11. Sullivan, "Books, Power, and the Development of Libraries"; David L. Sterling, "New York Patriarch: A Life of John Pintard, 1759–1844," Ph.D. diss., New York University, 1958; Dorothy C. Barck, ed., *Letters of John Pintard to His Daughter, Eliza Noel Pintard Davidson, 1816–1833,* 4 vols. (New York: New-York Historical Society, 1937–40).

12. Harry Elmer Barnes, *The Evolution of Penology in Pennsylvania: A Study in American Social History* (1927; reprint, Montclair, N.J.: Patterson Smith, 1969); Negley K. Teeters, *The Cradle of the Penitentiary: The Walnut Street Jail at Philadelphia* (Philadelphia: Pennsylvania Prison Society, 1935); LeRoy B. DePuy, "The Walnut Street Prison: Pennsylvania's First Penitentiary," *Pennsylvania History* 18 (April 1951): 2–16; and Blake McKelvey, *American Prisons: A History of Good Intentions* (Montclair, N.J.: Patterson Smith, 1977), 8–19.

13. McKelvey, *American Prisons,* 8; Teeters, *Cradle of the Penitentiary,* 29–32.

14. Orlando Lewis, *The Development of American Prison Customs, 1776–1845* (1922; reprint, Montclair, N.J.: Patterson Smith, 1967), 30.

15. *Reports of the Prison Discipline Society of Boston, 1826–1854* (1855; reprint, Montclair, N.J.: Patterson Smith, 1972), 1:28; McKelvey, *American Prisons,* 209.

16. Knapp, *Life of Thomas Eddy;* Ekirch, "Thomas Eddy and the Beginnings of Prison Reform in New York"; W. David Lewis, *From Newgate to*

Dannemora: The Rise of the Penitentiary in New York, 1796–1848 (Ithaca, N.Y.: Cornell University Press, 1965), 51–53.

17. Quoted in Orlando Lewis, *Development of American Prisons,* 44–45.

18. Ibid., 43–63; W. David Lewis, *From Newgate to Dannemora,* 29–53.

19. DePuy, "Walnut Street Prison," 23.

20. Ekirch, "Thomas Eddy and the Beginnings of Prison Reform in New York," 386ff.

21. W. A. Coffey, *Inside Out; or, An Interior View of the New-York State Prison; Together with Biographical Sketches of the Lives of Several of the Convicts* (New York: printed for the author, 1823), 134.

22. Caleb Lownes, *An Account of the Alteration and Present State of the Penal Laws of Pennsylvania* (Boston: Young and Minns, 1799).

23. Rothman, *Discovery of the Asylum,* 57–79.

24. Pessen, *Jacksonian America,* 81.

25. Mohl, *Poverty in New York,* 258–63; Rothman, *Discovery of the Asylum,* 58–59; Martin B. Miller, "Dread and Terror: The Creation of the State Penitentiaries in New York and Pennsylvania, 1788–1838," D. Criminology diss., University of California, Berkeley, 1980, 27.

26. Quoted in Frank Manuel, *Shapes of Philosophical History* (Stanford, Calif.: Stanford University Press, 1965), 91.

27. Stephen Allen, *Observations on Penitentiary Discipline, Addressed to William Roscoe, Esq. of Liverpool, England* (New York: J. C. Totten, 1827), 7.

28. *Reports of the Prison Discipline Society of Boston* (1826), 1:36.

29. The first recorded U.S. prison riot occurred in 1774 in the copper mine prison in Simsbury, Connecticut. See South Carolina Department of Corrections (Collective Violence Research Project), *Collective Violence in Correctional Institutions: A Search for Causes* (Columbia, S.C.: State Printing Co., 1973).

30. McKelvey, *American Prisons,* 16–17.

31. For biographical information on these reformers, see *Dictionary of American Biography* (New York: Charles Scribner's Sons, 1928–37). See also discussions in Rothman, *Discovery of the Asylum;* Orlando Lewis, *Development of American Prisons;* W. David Lewis, *From Newgate to Dannemora;* McKelvey, *American Prisons;* and Negley K. Teeters and John D. Shearer, *The Prison at Philadelphia Cherry Hill: The Separate System of Penal Discipline: 1829–1913* (New York: Columbia University Press, 1957).

32. Quoted in Norman Johnson, *The Human Cage: A Brief History of Prison Architecture* (New York: Walker and Co., 1973), 26–27.

33. Ibid., 40.

34. The best-known foreign advocate of this prison model was Alexis de Tocqueville, who toured American prisons in 1831. See Gustave de Beaumont and Alexis de Tocqueville, *On the Penitentiary System in the United States and Its Application in France,* translated with an introduction, notes, and additions by Francis Lieber (1833; reprint, Montclair, N.J.: Patterson Smith, 1976).

35. McKelvey, *American Prisons,* 44; Christopher R. X. Adamson, "Hard Labor: The Form and Function of Imprisonment in Nineteenth-Century America," Ph.D. diss., Princeton University, 1982.

36. Dorothea Dix, *Remarks on Prisons and Prison Discipline in the United States,* 2d ed. (1845; reprint, Montclair, N.J.: Patterson Smith, 1967); Helen Marshall, *Dorothea Dix: Forgotten Samaritan* (Chapel Hill, N.C.: University of North Carolina Press, 1937).

37. Robert S. Pickett, *House of Refuge: Origins of Juvenile Reform in New York State, 1815–1857* (Syracuse, N.Y.: Syracuse University Press, 1969); Mohl, *Poverty in New York*; Kaestle, *Pillars of the Republic*; Joseph M. Hawes, *Children in Urban Society; Juvenile Delinquency in Nineteenth-Century America* (New York: Oxford, 1971).

38. McKelvey, *American Prisons,* 52.

39. *Reports of the Prison Discipline Society of Boston* (1830) 1:34–35.

40. Nicole Hahn Rafter, *Partial Justice: Women in State Prisons, 1800–1935* (Boston: Northeastern University Press, 1985), 10.

41. For her phrenological views, see Marmaduke B. Sampson, *Rationale of Crime: And its Appropriate Treatment: Being a Treatise on Criminal Jurisprudence Considered in Relation to Cerebral Organization . . . with Notes and Illustrations by Eliza W. Farnham* (1846; reprint, Montclair, N.J.: Patterson Smith, 1973).

42. W. David Lewis, *From Newgate to Dannemora,* 237–50; W. David Lewis, "Eliza Woods Burnhans Farnham," in *Notable American Women 1607–1950,* vol. 1, ed. Edward T. James, Janet Wilson James, and Paul S. Boyer (Cambridge, Mass.: Belknap Press of Harvard University Press, 1971), 598–600; Rafter, *Partial Justice,* 17–20; Georgiana Bruce Kirby, *Years of Experience: An Autobiographical Narrative* (1887; reprint, New York: AMS Press, 1971); John Luckey, *Life in Sing Sing State Prison, as Seen in a Twelve Years' Chaplaincy* (New York: N. Tibbals, 1860); Estelle Freedman, *Their Sisters' Keepers: Women's Prison Reform in America, 1830–1930* (Ann Arbor: University of Michigan Press, 1981). Throughout the history of penal reform, most efforts have focused on the male criminal and not the female. Men, of course, have made up the vast majority of incarcerated felons. See the books by Rafter and Freedman.

43. John L. Thomas, "Romantic Reform in America, 1815–1865," *American Quarterly* 17 (Winter 1965): 656–81; M. J. Heale, "The Formative Years of the New York Prison Association, 1844–1862: A Case Study in Antebellum Reform," *New-York Historical Society Quarterly* 59 (October 1975): 320–47.

44. *First Report of the Prison Association of New York, December, 1844* (New York: Jared W. Bell, 1845), 13, 23.

45. Heale, "The Formative Years of the New York Prison Association," 341.

46. In general, see Samuel P. Hays, *The Response to Industrialism, 1885–1914* (Chicago: University of Chicago Press, 1957); Robert H. Wiebe, *The Search for Order, 1877–1920* (New York: Hill and Wang, 1967); and the bibliography in Arthur S. Link and Richard L. McCormick, *Progressivism* (Arlington Heights, Il.: Harland Davidson, 1983).

47. For biological determinism, see Arthur Fink, *Causes of Crime* (Philadelphia: University of Pennsylvania Press, 1938). For the environmental theories of the Progressives, see chapter 2 in this volume.

48. Mary Carpenter, *Reformatory Prison Discipline: As Developed by the Rt. Hon. Sir Walter Crofton in the Irish Convict Prisons* (1872; reprint, Montclair, N.J.: Patterson Smith, 1967).

49. *Twenty-Sixth Annual Report of the Executive Committee of the Prison Association of New York and Accompanying Documents for the Year 1870* (Albany, 1871); the appendix contains the *Transactions* of the National Congress on Penitentiary and Reformatory Discipline.

50. *Twenty-Sixth Annual Report of the . . . Prison Association of New York,* 18–20.

51. Ibid., 18.

52. Zebulon Reed Brockway, *Fifty Years of Prison Service: An Autobiography* (1912; reprint, Montclair, N.J.: Patterson Smith, 1969).

53. Enoch C. Wines, *The State of Prisons and of Child-Saving Institutions in the Civilized World* (1880; reprint, Montclair, N.J.: Patterson Smith, 1968), 120.

54. The first prison press was in the New York City Jail and published the first prison newspaper, *Forlorn Hope,* in 1800.

55. *Report of the Prison Discipline Society of Boston* (1830) 1:24–25.

56. Jacob Riis, *How the Other Half Lives* (1889; reprint, New York: Sagamore Press, 1957), 43, 45.

57. Wines, *State of Prisons,* 127.

58. McKelvey, *American Prisons,* 197–216; Paul W. Keve, *The History of Corrections in Virginia* (Charlottesville: University Press of Virginia, 1986); Mark T. Carleton, *Politics and Punishment: The History of the Louisiana State Penal System* (Baton Rouge: Louisiana State University Press, 1971); William C. Sneed, *A Report on the History and Mode of Management of the Kentucky Penitentiary From Its Origin, in 1798, to March 1, 1860* (Frankfort, Ky.: J. B. Major, 1860); Michael Stephen Hindus, *Prison and Plantation: Crime, Justice, and Authority in Massachusetts and South Carolina* (Chapel Hill: University of North Carolina Press, 1980); Clyde Crosley, *Unfolding Misconceptions: The Arkansas State Penitentiary, 1836–1986* (Arlington, Tx.: Liberal Arts Press, 1986).

59. McKelvey, *American Prisons,* 217–33; George Thomson, "History of Penal Institutions in the Rocky Mountain West, 1846–1900," Ph.D. diss., University of Colorado, 1965.

Chapter Two

1. Much of my discussion of the Progressive movement in general is based on the following works: Samuel P. Hays, *The Response to Industrialism, 1885–1914* (Chicago: University of Chicago Press, 1957); Robert H. Wiebe, *The Search for Order, 1877–1920* (New York: Hill and Wang, 1967); Paul Boyer, *Urban Masses and Moral Order in America, 1820–1920* (Cambridge, Mass.: Harvard University Press, 1978); William E. Leuchtenburg, *The Perils of Prosperity, 1914–32* (Chicago: University of Chicago Press, 1958); George E. Mowry, *The Era of Theodore Roosevelt, 1900–1912* (New York: Harper, 1958); Richard Hofstadter, *The Age of Reform: From Bryan to F.D.R.* (New York: Random House, 1955); R. Jackson Wilson, *In Quest of Community: Social Philosophy in the United States, 1860–1920* (New York: Wiley, 1968); Morton White, *Social Thought in America: The Revolt Against Formalism* (New York: Viking, 1949); Roy Lubove, *The Progressives and the Slums* (Pittsburgh: University of Pittsburgh Press, 1963); Robert H. Bremner, *From the Depths: The Discovery of Poverty in the United States* (New York: New York University Press, 1956); and especially for this chapter, David J. Rothman, *Conscience and Convenience: The Asylum and its Alternatives in Progressive America* (Boston: Little, Brown, 1980).

2. Charles A. Beard and Mary A. Beard, "Counter-Reformation and Asseveration," in *The American Spirit*, vol. 4 of *The Rise of Civilization* (New York: Macmillan, 1942), 384–481.

3. Mowry, *Era of Theodore Roosevelt*; William H. Harbaugh, *The Life and Times of Theodore Roosevelt*, rev. ed. (New York: Collier, 1963); Edmund Morris, *The Rise of Theodore Roosevelt* (New York: Coward, McCann, & Geoghegan, 1979).

4. Melvin Schiesl, *The Politics of Efficiency: Municipal Administration and Reform in America: 1880–1920* (Berkeley: University of California Press, 1977).

5. Arthur S. Link and Richard L. McCormick, *Progressivism* (Arlington Heights, Il.: Harland Davidson, 1983), 96.

6. U.S. Attorney General, *Survey of Release Procedures*, vol. 2, *Probation* (Washington, D.C.: U.S. Government Printing Office, 1939), 1–2, defined *probation* in this way: "As applied to modern courts, probation seeks to accomplish the rehabilitation of persons convicted of crime by returning them to society during a period of supervision, rather than sending them into the unnatural and too often socially unhealthful atmosphere of prisons and reformatories. . . . [Successful probation entails] an adequate investigation into the facts of the defendant's environment, character, and previous record; a wise selection by the court of the offenders capable of benefitting by the treatment, and a zealous but sympathetic prosecution of his duties but the supervisory officer."

7. U.S. Attorney General, *Survey of Release Procedures*, vol. 4, *Parole* (Washington, D.C.: U.S. Government Printing Office, 1939), 2, defined *parole*

in this way: "A parole does not release the parolee from custody, it does not discharge or absolve him from the penal consequences of his act; it does not mitigate his punishment; it does not wash away the stain or remit the penalty; it does not reverse the judgment of the court or declare him to have been innocent or affect the record against him. . . . Unlike a pardon, it is not an act of grace or of mercy, of clemency or leniency. The granting of parole is merely permission to a prisoner to serve a portion of his sentence outside the walls of the prison. He continues to be in the custody of the authorities, both legally and actually, and is still under restraint. The sentence is in full force and at any time when he does not comply with the conditions upon which he is released, or does not conduct himself properly, he may be returned, for his own good and in the public interest."

8. Rothman, *Conscience and Convenience,* 44; John Augustus, *John Augustus, First Probation Officer* (1852; reprint, Montclair, N.J.: Patterson Smith, 1972).

9. Blake McKelvey, *American Prisons: A History of Good Intentions* (Montclair, N.J.: Patterson Smith, 1977), 247–48.

10. Harry Elmer Barnes and Negley K. Teeters, *New Horizons in Criminology: The American Crime Problem* (New York: Prentice-Hall, 1943), 373–90.

11. Allen F. Davis, *Spearheads for Reform: The Social Settlements and the Progressive Movement* (New York: Oxford University Press, 1967); Charles Lindner and Margaret R. Savarese, "The Evolution of Probation: Early Salaries, Qualifications, and Hiring Practices," *Federal Probation* 48 (March 1984): 3–10; "The Evolution of Probation: The Historical Contributions of the Volunteer," *Federal Probation* 48 (June 1984): 3–10; "The Evolution of Probations: University Settlement and the Beginning of Statutory Probation in New York City," *Federal Probation* 48 (September 1984): 3–12; "The Evolution of Proba- tion: University Settlement and Its Pioneering Role in Probation Work," *Federal Probation* 38 (December 1984): 3–13.

12. Lindner and Savarese, "Early Salaries, Qualifications, and Hiring Prac- tices," "University Settlement and Its Pioneering Role in Probation Work," 5–6.

13. Rothman, *Conscience and Convenience,* 92–103.

14. Barnes and Teeters, *New Horizons in Criminology,* 376.

15. Ibid., 384–385.

16. *Survey of Release Procedures,* vol. 2, *Probation.*

17. Mary Carpenter, *Our Convicts,* 2 vols. (1864; reprint, Montclair, N.J.: Patterson Smith, 1969); Alexander Maconochie, *Thoughts on Convict Manage- ment, and other Subjects Connected with the Australian Penal Colonies* (Hobart Town: J. C. Macdougall, 1839).

18. *Survey of Release Procedures,* vol. 4, *Parole,* 2.

19. Barnes and Teeters, *New Horizons in Criminology,* 815.

20. Philip Jenkins, "The Radicals and the Rehabilitative Ideal, 1890–1930," *Criminology* 20 (November 1982): 347–72.

21. Ibid.

22. Speaking at a 1939 parole conference in Washington, D.C.; quoted in Barnes and Teeters, *New Horizons in Criminology*, 825.

23. New York State, *Report of the Special Commission on the Parole Problem* (1930), 12.

24. For a full discussion of the warden's role, see Rothman, *Conscience and Convenience*, 183–87.

25. Barnes and Teeters, *New Horizons in Criminology*, 828.

26. National Conference on Parole, Washington, D.C., Committee on Standards and Procedures, *Proceedings* (Leavenworth, Kans., 1940).

27. Harry Elmer Barnes, *The Story of Punishment*, 2d ed. (Montclair, N.J.: Patterson Smith, 1972), 212.

28. On Osborne's life, see Frank Tannenbaum, *Osborne of Sing Sing* (Chapel Hill, N.C.: University of North Carolina Press, 1933).

29. Donald Lowrie, *My Life in Prison* (New York: Mitchell Kennerley, 1912).

30. Thomas Mott Osborne, *Within Prison Walls* (1914; reprint, Montclair, N.J.: Patterson Smith, 1969).

31. Thomas Mott Osborne, *Prisons and Common Sense* (New York: Lippincott, 1924), 57ff.

32. Nicole Hahn Rafter, *Partial Justice: Women in State Prisons, 1800–1935* (Boston: Northeastern University Press, 1985), 69ff; Katherine B. Davis, "Treatment of the Female Offender," in Seventh New York State Conference of Charities and Correction, *Proceedings, 1906,* in New York State Board of Charities, *Annual Report, 1906,* 785–90; Katherine B. Davis, "The New York State Reformatory for Women," *Survey* 25 (1911): 851–54; Estelle B. Freedman, *Their Sisters' Keepers: Women's Prison Reform in America, 1830–1930* (Ann Arbor: University of Michigan, 1981).

33. National Commission on Law Observance and Enforcement, *Penal Institutions, Probation and Parole* (1931; reprint, Montclair, N.J.: Patterson Smith, 1968).

34. *Baltimore American,* 1 November 1822.

35. For a detailed examination of the methods of the prison labor system, see Christopher R. X. Adamson, "Hard Labor: The Form and Function of Imprisonment in Nineteenth-Century America," Ph.D. diss., Princeton University, 1982.

36. Rothman, *Conscience and Convenience*, 137.

37. *Journal of Criminal Law and Criminology* (January–February, 1938), 627.

38. Sanford Bates, *Prisons and Beyond* (1936; reprint, Freeport, N.Y.: Books for Libraries Press, 1971).

39. Donald Clemmer, *The Prison Community* (1940; reprint, New York: Rinehart, 1958).

Chapter Three

1. The Trenton riots are detailed in Gresham M. Sykes, *The Society of Captives: A Study of a Maximum Security Prison* (Princeton, N.J.: Princeton University Press, 1958), 112ff.
2. Ibid., 118–19.
3. This account is based largely on Vernon Fox, *Violence behind Bars* (New York: Vintage Press, 1956), and John Barlow Martin, *Break Down the Walls* (New York: Ballantine Books, 1954).
4. Martin, *Break Down the Walls,* 86.
5. The incidents at Angola are covered in Mark T. Carleton, *Politics and Punishment: History of the Louisiana State Penal System* (Baton Rouge: Louisiana State University Press, 1971).
6. See, for instance, John Conley, "A History of the Oklahoma Penal System, 1907–1967," Ph.D. diss., Michigan State University, 1977.
7. Federal Bureau of Prisons, *Annual Report* (Washington, D.C.: U.S. Government Printing Office, 1948), 3.
8. *A Statement concerning Causes, Preventive Measures, and Methods of Controlling Prison Riots and Disturbances. Prepared by the Committee on Riots under the Auspices of the American Prison Association* (New York: American Prison Association, 1953).
9. Ibid.; Martin, *Break Down the Walls,* 222.
10. Donald Clemmer, "Observations on Imprisonment as a Source of Criminality," *Journal of Criminal Law and Criminology* 41 (September–October 1950): 311–19.
11. Ibid., 319.
12. Lloyd W. McCorkle and Richard Korn, "Resocialization within the Walls," *Annals of the American Academy of Political and Social Science* 293 (May 1954): 88–98.
13. Richard Korn and Lloyd W. McCorkle, *Criminology and Penology* (New York: Holt, Rinehart and Winston, 1961), 530.
14. Clarence Schrag, "Leadership Among Prison Inmates," *American Sociological Review* 19 (February 1954): 37–42.
15. Richard Quinney, *The Social Reality of Crime* (Boston: Little, Brown, 1970).
16. Sykes, *The Society of Captives,* 109ff.
17. Neil Smelser, "The Theory of Collective Behavior," in South Carolina Department of Corrections (Collective Violence Research Project), *Collective Violence in Correctional Institutions: A Search for Causes* (Columbia: S.C.: State Printing Co., 1973); Neil J. Smelser, *Theory of Collective Behavior* (New York: The Free Press, 1962); A. Smith, "The Conflict Theory of Riots," in South Carolina Department of Corrections, *Collective Violence in Correctional Institutions*; Steven D. Dillingham and Reid H. Montgomery, Jr., "Prison Riots: A Cor-

rections' Nightmare Since 1774," in Michael Braswell, Steven Dillingham, and Reid Montgomery, Jr., *Prison Violence in America* (Cincinnati: Anderson Publishing Co., 1985), 19–35.

18. Nathan Leopold, *Life Plus Ninety-Nine Years* (New York: Doubleday, 1957), 214.

19. *Shake down* in a prison means that the administration is tightening up rule enforcement against contraband and illicit activities. Prisoners are confined to their cells while guards search and seize weapons, drugs, and the like.

20. James B. Jacobs, *Stateville: The Penitentiary in Mass Society* (Chicago: University of Chicago Press, 1977), 30.

21. *Chicago Tribune,* quoted in Jacobs, *Stateville,* 44.

22. Jacobs, *Stateville,* 46.

Chapter Four

1. Paul W. Tappan, *Crime, Justice and Correction* (New York: McGraw-Hill, 1960), 646.

2. American Prison Association, (Committee on Classification and Case Work) *Handbook on Classification in Correctional Institutions* (New York: American Prison Association, 1947), 2–3; *A Manual of Correctional Standards,* rev. ed. (New York: American Correctional Association, 1959).

3. Norman Fenton, "The Process of Reception in the Adult Correctional System," *The Annals* 293 (May 1954): 52–53.

4. Alfred C. Schnur, "The New Penology: Fact or Fiction?" *Journal of Criminal Law, Criminology and Police Science* 49 (November–December 1958): 331–34.

5. Malcolm Braly, *False Starts: A Memoir of San Quentin and Other Prisons* (New York: Penguin, 1977), 158.

6. Quoted in Francis A. Allen, *The Decline of the Rehabilitative Ideal: Penal Policy and Public Purpose* (New Haven, Conn.: Yale University Press, 1981), 124, n. 63.

7. Braly, *False Starts,* 161.

8. Ibid., 178.

9. Janet Harris, *Crisis in Corrections: The Prison Problem* (New York: McGraw-Hill, 1973), 105.

10. Richard R. Korn and Lloyd W. McCorkle, *Criminology and Penology* (New York: Henry Holt, 1959), 576; Lloyd W. McCorkle, Albert Elias, and F. Lovell Bixby, *The Highfields Story: A Unique Experiment in the Treatment of Juvenile Delinquents* (New York: Henry Holt, 1958); H. Ashley Weeks, *Youthful Offenders at Highfields* (Ann Arbor: University of Michigan Press, 1958).

11. LaMar Emprey, "Juvenile Justice Reform: Diversion, Due Process, and

Deinstitutionalization," in Lloyd Ohlin, ed., *Prisoners in America* (Englewood Cliffs, N.J.: Prentice-Hall, 1973), 13–48, contests these findings.

12. Korn and McCorkle, *Criminology and Penology,* 540.

13. F. Lovell Bixby and Lloyd W. McCorkle, "A Recorded Presentation of a Program of Guided Group Interaction in New Jersey's Correctional Institutions," *Proceedings of the Seventy-Eighth Annual Congress of Correction of the American Prison Association* (Boston, 1948); quoted in Korn and McCorkle, *Criminology and Penology,* 569–70.

14. Lloyd W. McCorkle, "Group Therapy in the Treatment of Offenders," *Federal Probation* 16 (December 1952): 22–27.

15. Malcolm Braly, *On the Yard* (Boston: Little, Brown, 1967), 103–104.

16. *Struggle for Justice. A Report on Crime and Punishment in America, prepared for the American Friends Service Committee* (New York: Hill and Wang, 1971), 90.

17. John R. Wald Co., *Correctional Industries: State Use Sales, 1950–1970* (Huntingdon, Pa., 1971).

18. Karl Menninger, *The Crime of Punishment* (New York: Viking, 1968), 231–32; quoted in Jessica Mitford, *Kind and Unusual Punishment: The Prison Business* (New York: Alfred A. Knopf, 1973), 98–99.

19. John Irwin, *The Felon* (Englewood Cliffs, N.J.: Prentice-Hall, 1970), 52.

20. Robert J. Minton, Jr., ed., *Inside Prison American Style* (New York: Random House, 1971), 156.

21. Braly, *False Starts,* 196.

22. Ibid., 251–52.

23. *Deterrent Effects of Criminal Sanctions,* Progress Report of the Assembly Committee on Criminal Procedure (Sacramento, May 1968), 71; quoted in Mitford, *Kind and Unusual Punishment,* 93–94.

24. Schnur, "The New Penology: Fact or Fiction?" 331–34.

25. Korn and McCorkle, *Criminology and Penology,* 588.

Chapter Five

1. Zebulon Brockway, *Fifty Years of Prison Service* (1912; reprint, Montclair, N.J.: Patterson Smith, 1969).

2. Edwin H. Sutherland and Donald R. Cressey, *Principles of Criminology,* 7th ed. (New York: Lippincott, 1966), 81–82.

3. Richard Cloward and Lloyd E. Ohlin, *Delinquency and Opportunity* (Glencoe, Ill.: The Free Press, 1961).

4. Robert Merton, "Social Structure and Anomie," *American Sociological Review* 3 (1938): 672–82; *Social Theory and Social Structure* (Glencoe, Ill.: The Free Press, 1957).

5. Robert Burgess and Ronald Akers, "A Differential Association-Reinforcement Theory of Criminal Behavior," *Social Problems* 14 (1966): 128–47; also see Akers's later work, *Deviant Behavior: A Social Learning Approach* (Belmont, Calif.: Wadsworth, 1977).

6. Edward Lemert, *Social Pathology* (New York: McGraw-Hill, 1951).

7. Albert Cohen, *Delinquent Boys: The Culture of the Gang* (Glencoe, Ill.: The Free Press, 1955); a similar view of delinquent subcultures was developed by Walter B. Miller in "Lower Class Cultures as a Generating Milieu of Gang Delinquency," *Journal of Social Issues* 14 (1958): 5–19. See also David J. Bordua, "Delinquent Subcultures: Sociological Interpretations of Gang Delinquency," *Annals of the American Academy of Political and Social Science* 338 (November 1961): 119–36.

8. Don G. Gibbons, *Changing the Lawbreaker: The Treatment of Delinquents and Criminals* (Englewood Cliffs, N.J.: Prentice-Hall, 1965), 157.

9. See Stanton Samenow, *Inside the Criminal Mind* (New York: Times Books, 1984), and Samuel Yochelson and Stanton Samenow, *The Criminal Personality*, 2 vols. (New York: Jason Aronson, 1976–77).

10. Helen L. Witmer and Edith Tufts, *The Effectiveness of Delinquency Prevention Programs*, U.S. Children's Bureau Publication no. 350 (Washington, D.C.: U.S. Government Printing Office, 1954), 11; see also Clifford R. Shaw and Henry D. McKay, *Juvenile Delinquency and Urban Areas* (Chicago: University of Chicago Press, 1942), and Solomon Kobrin, "The Chicago Area Project—A 25-Year Assessment," *Annals of the American Academy of Political and Social Science* 322 (March 1959): 19–29.

11. See Sophia M. Robison, "Why Juvenile Delinquency Preventive Programs are Ineffective," *Federal Probation* 25 (December 1961): 34–41.

12. Sanger B. Powers, "Off-Grounds Activities Present an Opportunity for Correctional Institutions," *Federal Probation* 31 (June 1967): 11–15.

13. See John Irwin, *Prisons in Turmoil* (Boston: Little, Brown, 1980), 156–57.

14. American Friends Service Committee, *Struggle for Justice* (New York: Hill and Wang, 1971), 91.

15. Malcolm X and Alex Haley, *The Autobiography of Malcolm X* (New York: Macmillan, 1965), 183.

16. Quoted in Janet Harris, *Crisis in Corrections: The Prison Problem* (New York: McGraw-Hill, 1973), 129.

17. Ibid.

18. Donald R. Cressey, "Adult Felons in Prison," in Lloyd E. Ohlin, ed., *Prisoners in America* (Englewood Cliffs, N.J.: Prentice-Hall, 1973), 117–50.

19. The President's Commission on Law Enforcement and the Administration of Justice, *Task Force Report: Corrections* (Washington, D.C.: U.S. Government Printing Office, 1967), 4.

20. Ibid., 7.

21. Ibid., 9.

22. Ibid., 11.

23. James Vorenberg, "The Crime Commission's Report," *Federal Probation* 31 (June 1967): 3–6.

24. Ibid., 12.

25. Brian Glick, "Change through the Courts," in Erik Olin Wright, *The Politics of Punishment: A Critical Analysis of Prisons in America* (New York: Harper and Row, 1973), 281–312.

26. Ibid.

27. Robert J. Minton, Jr., ed., *Inside Prison American Style* (New York: Random House, 1971), 103.

28. See Francis A. Allen, *The Decline of the Rehabilitative Ideal: Penal Policy and Social Purpose* (New Haven: Yale University Press, 1981), 73.

29. South Carolina Department of Corrections (Collective Violence Research Project), *Collective Violence in Correctional Institutions: A Search for Causes* (Columbia, S.C.: State Printing Co., 1973).

30. Gene Kassebaum, David A. Ward, and Daniel M. Wilner, *Prison Treatment and Parole Survival* (New York: Wiley, 1971); Leslie T. Wilkins, *Evaluation of Penal Measures* (Berkeley: University of California Press, 1969); Douglas Lipton, Robert Martinson, and Judith Wilks, *The Effectiveness of Correctional Treatment* (New York: Praeger, 1975). The 1975 study is discussed in more detail in chapter 6.

Chapter Six

1. *Attica: The Official Report of the New York State Special Commission on Attica,* the McKay commission report (New York: Bantam, 1972), photograph no. 29.

2. Quoted in Jessica Mitford, *Kind and Unusual Punishment: The Prison Business* (New York: Alfred A. Knopf, 1973), 233.

3. Min S. Yee, *The Melancholy History of Soledad Prison* (New York: Harper's Magazine Press, 1973), 24.

4. Erik Olin Wright, *The Politics of Punishment: A Critical Analysis of Prisons in America* (New York: Harper and Row, 1973), 100–101.

5. Ibid., 121.

6. Ibid., 107.

7. For some of the literature on the Attica riot see the McKay commission report; Tom Wicker, *A Time to Die* (New York: Quadrangle/New York Times, 1975); Norval Morris and Gordon Hawkins, "Attica Revisited: The Prospect for Prison Reform," *Psychiatric Annals* 4 (1974): 21–42; Sue Mahan, "An 'Orgy of Brutality' at Attica and the 'Killing Ground' at Santa Fe: A Comparison of Prison Riots," in Michael Braswell, Steven Dillingham, and Reid Montgomery, Jr., eds., *Prison Violence in America* (Cincinnati: Anderson Publishing Co., 1985), 73–87;

Russell G. Oswald, *Attica—My Own Story* (New York: Doubleday, 1972); Malcolm Bell, *The Turkey Shoot* (New York: Grove Press, 1985); William R. Coons, *Attica Diary* (New York: Stein and Day, 1972); Richard X. Clark, *The Brothers of Attica* (New York: Links, 1973); and the daily news accounts in the *New York Times*.

8. McKay commission report, 141.

9. Ibid., 150.

10. Ibid., 165.

11. Ibid., 230. The injunction concerned only events on 9 September; this quote was made on 10 September.

12. Ibid., 323–24.

13. Ibid., 281.

14. Ibid., 281.

15. Richard Quinney, *Critique of Legal Order: Crime Control in Capitalist Society* (Boston: Little, Brown, 1973), 16.

16. David Gordon, "Class and the Economics of Crime," *Review of Radical Political Economy* 3 (171): 51.

17. *Lockdown* means that prisoners are confined most of the day to their cells.

18. Douglas Lipton, Robert Martinson, and Judith Wilks, *The Effectiveness of Correctional Treatment* (New York: Praeger, 1975).

19. "What Works? Questions and Answers about Prison Reform," *Public Interest* (Spring 1974): 23–54.

20. See chapter 5 for theories of differential association.

21. American Friends Service Committee, *Struggle for Justice* (New York: Hill and Wang, 1971), 9.

22. Ibid., 33.

23. National Advisory Commission on Criminal Justice Standards and Goals, *Corrections* (Washington, D.C.: U.S. Government Printing Office, 1973), 8.

24. Ibid., 1.

25. Wright, *Politics of Punishment*, 341.

26. David Greenberg, "Problems in Community Corrections," *Issues in Criminology* (Spring 1975): 5.

27. Margaret Warner Cahalan with Lee Ann Parson, *Historical Corrections Statistics in the United States, 1850–1984*, U.S. Department of Justice, Bureau of Statistics Report (Rockville, Md.: Westat, 1986).

28. Ibid., 30.

Chapter Seven

1. See, for instance, Sue Mahan, "An 'Orgy of Brutality' at Attica and the 'Killing Ground' at Santa Fe: A Comparison of Prison Riots," in Michael Braswell,

Steven Dillingham, and Reid Montgomery, Jr., eds., *Prison Violence in America* (Cincinnati: Anderson Publishing Co., 1985): 73–87.

2. For the New Mexico riot, see Michael S. Serrill and Peter Katel, "The Anatomy of a Riot: The Facts behind New Mexico's Bloody Ordeal," *Corrections Magazine* 6 (1980): 6–16, 20–24; Mark Colvin, "The New Mexico Prison Riot," *Social Problems* 29 (1982): 449–63; Wilbert Rideau and Billy Sinclair, "The Lessons of Santa Fe: Two Louisiana Lifers Look at the Bloodiest Riot in American History," *Dallas Times Herald,* 2 February 1981; Roger Morris, *The Devil's Butcher Shop: The New Mexico Prison Uprising* (New York: Franklin Watts, 1982); *Albuquerque Journal and Tribune* [New Mexico], 3 February–15 June 1980.

3. Attorney General of New Mexico, *Report of the Attorney General on the February 2 and 3, 1980, Riot at the Penitentiary of New Mexico* (Santa Fe: Office of the Attorney General of New Mexico, 1980), part 1, 26.

4. Morris, *The Devil's Butcher Shop,* 100–101.

5. Ibid., 105.

6. See note 3.

7. *Albuquerque Journal,* 16 May 1981.

8. *New York Times,* 9 October 1983.

9. *New York Times,* 2 October 1983.

10. *New York Times,* 23 November 1983.

11. *U.S. News & World Report,* 28 November 1977, 76–79.

12. Ibid., 77.

13. Jonathan D. Casper, David Brereton, and David Neal, *The Implementation of the California Determinate Sentencing Law* (Washington, D.C.: U.S. Department of Justice, 1982), 13.

14. Ibid., 15.

15. Ibid., 2.

16. Henry R. Glick, "Mandatory Sentencing: The Politics of the New Criminal Justice," *Federal Probation* 43 (March 1979): 5–9, quoting Eugene Z. DuBose, "Criminal Sentencing: Point and Counterpoint," *Journal of Criminal Law and Criminology* 65 (March 1974), 128.

17. The following account is based on Casper, Brereton, and Neal, *Implementation,* and Richard A. McGee, "California's New Determinate Sentencing Law," *Federal Probation* 42 (March 1978): 3–10.

18. Sol Rubin, "New Sentencing Laws in the 1970s," *Federal Probation* 33 (June 1979): 1–8.

19. U.S. Sentencing Commission, *Guidelines Manual* (Washington, D.C.: U.S. Government Printing Office, 1988), plus updates.

20. Norval Morris, *The Future of Imprisonment* (Chicago: University of Chicago Press, 1974), 2; see also Benjamin Frank, "The American Prison: End of an Era," *Federal Probation* 33 (September 1979): 3–9.

21. Frank, "American Prison," 8.

22. Glick, "Mandatory Sentencing."

23. Minnesota's law requires that a maximum number of prisoners be set and that when that maximum is reached some have to be released before more can enter prison; see Minnesota Sentencing Guidelines Commission, *Minnesota Sentencing Guidelines and Commentary* (St. Paul: Minnesota Sentencing Guidelines Commission, 1987); Andrew E. Doom, Connie M. Roehrich, and Thomas H. Zoet, "Sentencing Guidelines in Minnesota: The View from the Trenches," *Federal Probation* 52 (December 1988): 34–38. Connecticut law mandates the release of 10 percent of its inmates if the system exceeds 110 percent of capacity for thirty consecutive days.

24. Barton L. Ingraham and Charles F. Wellford, "The Totality of Conditions Test in Eighth-Amendment Legislation," in Stephen D. Gottfredson and Sean McConville, *America's Correctional Crisis: Prison Populations and Public Policy* (New York: Greenwood Press, 1987): 13–35.

25. John J. DiIulio, Jr., *Governing Prisons: A Comparative Study of Correctional Management* (New York: The Free Press, 1987), 212–16.

26. Ingraham and Wellford, "The Totality of Conditions Test in Eighth-Amendment Litigation," 29.

27. Don M. Gottfredson, "The Problem of Crowding: A System Out of Control," in Gottfredson and McConville, *America's Correctional Crisis,* 137–59.

28. Todd R. Clear and Patricia M. Harris, "The Costs of Incarceration," in Gottfredson and McConville, *America's Correctional Crisis,* 37–55.

29. New York City Comptroller, *Report* (1988), 6.

30. Joan Mullen, "State Responses to Prison Crowding: The Politics of Change," in Gottfredson and McConville, *America's Correctional Crisis,* 79–109.

31. U.S. Congress, Office of Technology Assessment, *Criminal Justice: New Technologies and the Constitution* (Washington, D.C.: U.S. Government Printing Office, 1988), 33.

32. Ibid., 34.

33. Ibid., 35.

34. *New York Times,* 3 February 1985.

35. President's Commission on Privatization, *Privatization: Toward More Effective Government* (Washington, D.C.: The Commission, 1988).

36. Ibid., 149–51.

37. Ira P. Robbins, "Privatization of Corrections: Defining the Issues," *Federal Probation* 50 (September 1986), 26.

38. Ibid.

39. Ibid., 28.

40. See, for instance, Joan Mullen, Kent J. Chabotar, and Deborah M. Carrow, *The Privatization of Corrections,* U.S. Department of Justice, National Institute of Justice Report (Washington, D.C.: U.S. Government Printing Office, 1985).

Selected Bibliography

I have included here some of the more pertinent books in the field, as well as doctoral dissertations that contain information not available elsewhere. Many, but not all, of these sources are cited in the notes. The most important works are discussed in the text.

American Correctional Association. *The American Prison: From the Beginning . . . A Pictorial History.* College Park, Md.: American Correctional Association, 1983. An illustrated history.

American Friends Service Committee. *Struggle for Justice.* New York: Hill and Wang, 1971. The Quaker critique of the penal system.

Baker, J. E. *Prisoner Participation in Prison Power.* Metuchen, N.J., 1985. A study of prisoners' sharing power.

Barnes, Harry Elmer, and Negley K. Teeters. *New Horizons in Criminology: The American Crime Problem.* New York: Prentice-Hall, 1943. The classic Progressive view.

———. *The Evolution of Penology in Pennsylvania: A Study in American Social History.* Montclair, N.J.: Patterson Smith, 1968. Originally published in 1927.

Berkman, Ronald. *Opening the Gates: The Rise of the Prisoners' Movement.* Lexington, Mass.: D.C. Heath, 1979. Introduction to the changes in prisoners' perception of convict rights.

Cohen, Stanley. *Visions of Social Control: Crime, Punishment and Classification.* Oxford: Polity Press, 1985. Advocates short-term, humane conditions and a system of anarchy for a long-term solution.

Currie, Elliott. *Confronting Crime: An American Challenge.* New York: Pantheon, 1985. Calls for more humane alternatives to imprisonment.

Feinman, Clarice. "Imprisoned Women: A History of the Women Incarcerated in New York City, 1932–1975." Ph.D. diss., New York University, 1976.

Freedman, Estelle B. *Their Sisters' Keepers: Women's Prison Reform in America, 1830–1930.* Ann Arbor: University of Michigan Press, 1981. The basic work on early prison reform for women.

Foucault, Michel. *Discipline and Punish: The Birth of the Prison.* New York: Pantheon, 1977. An original and provocative but unreliable work.

Gamberg, Herbert, and Anthony Thomson. *The Illusion of Prison Reform: Corrections in Canada.* New York: Peter Lang, 1984. Criticism of Canadian prison reform.

Garland, David, and Peter Young. *The Power to Punish: Contemporary Penality and Social Analysis.* Atlantic Highlands, N.J.: 1983. Insightful essays on social control, community corrections, Michel Foucault, Emile Durkheim, and other topics.

Glaser, Daniel. *The Effectiveness of a Prison and Parole System.* Indianapolis: Bobbs-Merrill, 1964. A study of variables leading to criminal recidivism.

Goffman, Erving. *Asylums.* Garden City, N.Y.: Anchor Books, 1961. A classic work on the mental categories of the institutionalized.

Gottfredson, Stephen D., and Sean McConville, eds. *America's Correctional Crisis: Prison Populations and Public Policy.* New York: Greenwood, 1987. Important essays on the costs of incarceration and on prison crowding.

Helfman, Harold M. "A History of Penal, Correctional and Reformatory Institutions in Michigan, 1839–1889." Ph.D. diss., University of Michigan, 1947.

Irwin, John. *Prisons in Turmoil.* Boston: Little, Brown, 1980. An informative critique by a sociologist and ex-convict.

Jacobs, James B. *New Perspectives on Prisons and Imprisonment.* Ithaca, N.Y.: Cornell University Press, 1983. Good, incisive essays on prisoners' rights and prison subcultures, among other topics.

Jackson, Bruce. *Law and Disorder: Criminal Justice in America.* Urbana, Ill.: University of Illinois Press, 1984. Biting criticism of the American criminal justice system as a whole.

Johnston, Norman. *The Human Cage: A Brief History of Prison Architecture.* New York: Walker, 1973. One of the few books devoted solely to prison architecture.

Jones, David. *History of Criminology: A Philosophical Perspective.* New York: Greenwood Press, 1986. A good, brief introduction to the major theories of crime and punishment.

Lewis, Orlando. *The Development of American Prison Customs, 1776–1845.* Montclair, N.J.: Patterson Smith, 1967. Although originally published in 1922, this work still contains much useful information.

Lewis, W. David. *From Newgate to Dannemora: The Rise of the Penitentiary in New York, 1796–1848.* Ithaca, N.Y.: Cornell University Press, 1965. The best study on the early development of the Auburn and Sing Sing penitentiary model.

Lipton, Douglas, Robert Martinson, and Judith Wilks. *The Effectiveness of Correctional Treatment.* New York: Praeger, 1975. The important study that illustrated the failure of treatment methods.

McCarthy, Belinda, ed. *Intermediate Punishments: Intensive Supervision, Home Confinement and Electronic Surveillance.* Monsey, N.Y.: Criminal Justice Press, 1987. Essays on the new technologies and methods of surveillance.

McDonald, Douglas Corry. *Punishment without Walls: Community Service Sentences in New York City.* New Brunswick, N.J.: Rutgers University Press, 1986. A study of sentencing reform in New York City.

McGee, Richard A. *Prisons and Politics.* Lexington, Mass.: D.C. Heath, 1981. A study by the former California director of corrections.

McKelvey, Blake. *American Prisons: A History of Good Intentions.* Montclair, N.J.: Patterson Smith, 1977. One of the more thoughtful surveys of American prison history.

Martin, Steve J., and Sheldon Ekland-Olson. *Texas Prisons: The Walls Came Tumbling Down.* Austin: Texas Monthly Press, 1987. Recent history of the Texas penal system.

Melossi, Dario, and Massimo Pavarini. *The Prison and the Origins of the Penitentiary System.* London: Macmillan 1981. On prisons in Italy.

Messinger, Sheldon. "Strategies of Control." Ph.D. diss., University of California, Berkeley, 1969. History of the indeterminate sentence.

Mitford, Jessica. *Kind and Unusual Punishment: The Prison Business.* New York: Alfred A. Knopf, 1973. Biting criticism of the penal system as a whole.

Pontell, Henry N. *A Capacity to Punish: The Ecology of Crime and Punishment.* Bloomington: Indiana University Press, 1984. A criticism of criminal justice under conservative governments; calls for the use of the criminal justice system only as a last resort.

Rothman, David J. *The Discovery of the Asylum: Social Order and Disorder in the New Republic.* Boston: Little, Brown, 1971.

———. *Conscience and Convenience: The Asylum and its Alternatives in Progressive America.* Boston: Little, Brown, 1980. Rothman's two books are the best introduction to the history of prisons and asylums from their inception through the Progressive era.

Rusche, Georg, and Otto Kirchheimer. *Punishment and Social Structure.* New York: Russell and Russell, 1968. Originally published in 1939, this is the classic statement of the economic causes of crime and punishment.

Saney, Parvis. *Crime and Culture in America: A Comparative Perspective.* New York: Greenwood, 1986. Takes the current view that prisons are for punishment and that rehabilitation should be the personal choice of the offender.

Scull, Andrew. *Decarceration: Community Treatment and the Deviant: A Radical View.* Englewood Cliffs, N.J.: Prentice-Hall, 1977. On contemporary reform movements that seek the deinstitutionalization of the deviant.

Sutherland, Edwin H., and Donald R. Cressey. *Principles of Criminology.* 7th ed. New York: J. B. Lippincott, 1966. The classic textbook in the field; outlines the theory of differential association.

Suvak, Daniel. *Memoirs of America Prisons: An Annotated Bibliography.* Metuchen, N.J.: Scarecrow, 1979. Memoirs written in prison are invaluable sources of institutional history. Suvak lists almost five hundred titles written by civil prisoners, as well as hundreds more by military prisoners and others.

Tappan, Paul W. *Crime, Justice and Correction.* New York: McGraw Hill, 1960. The basic view from the late 1950s.

Thomas, Charles W. *Corrections in America: Problems of Past and Present.* Newbury Park, Calif.: Sage Publications, 1987. A primer.

Index